101 CROSS STITCH CARD DESIGNS

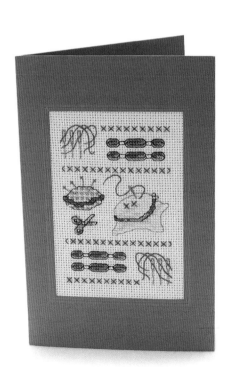

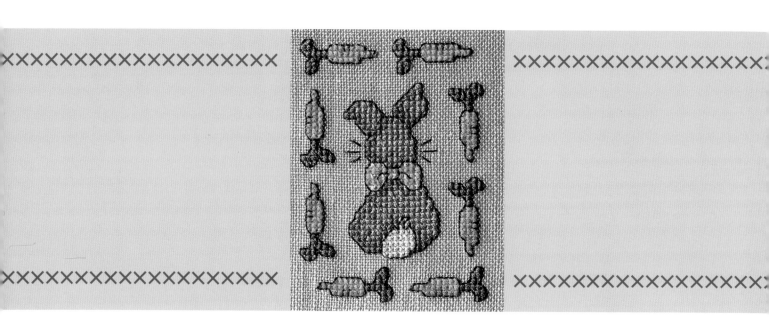

hamlyn

101 CROSS STITCH CARD DESIGNS

Maria Diaz

First published in Great Britain in 2003 by Hamlyn, a division of Octopus Publishing Group Ltd 2-4 Heron Quays, London E14 4JP

Copyright © Octopus Publishing Group Ltd 2003

ISBN 0 600 60906 5

A CIP catalogue record for this book is available from the British Library

Printed and bound in China

10 9 8 7 6 5 4 3 2 1

All cross stitch projects designed by Maria Diaz, except for the following:

Lesley Grant 18, 59, 66
Lucie Heaton 46, 67, 90, 93
Steven Jenkins 19, 65
Penelope Randall 12, 13, 35, 42
Jane Rimmer 34
Julia Tidmarsh 33, 53
Sue Whiting 26, 58
Lynda Whittle 36, 91

Contents

Celebrations

Hobbies and Special Interests

Children's Themes

Flora and Fauna

Introduction

Cross stitch is one of the most popular of all forms of needlecraft. It first appeared in the 16th century, and the technique was traditionally used in samplers that were worked by young embroiderers as a means of perfecting their skills and as a reference for stitches and patterns. Back in vogue once more, cross stitch is easy to learn, and the results appear quickly. The equipment you need is minimal, so small projects are completely portable and can be taken almost anywhere.

Cross stitch can be an absorbing hobby, and once you are hooked it will not be long before you have filled all the available wall space in your home with the fruits of your labours. When you have mastered the basic stitch, you will find that cross stitch is a wonderful way of creating pictures. If you can read a chart, then you can tackle any of the designs in this book with complete confidence.

Beginners may wish to start by reading the materials and techniques section at the back of this book (see pages 104–9). Here we cover all the basic information required by the novice stitcher, ranging from choosing fabrics and how to form individual stitches to how to mount finished projects with style.

Stitching greetings cards for friends and family is an excellent way to satisfy your need to sew, and at the same time you will be creating something a little more personal with which to celebrate a family occasion or special event. In this book we have tried to provide original designs that are suitable for every

left: Christmas time presents an ideal opportunity for prolific stitching. Your festive greetings will be a joy for friends and family to receive.

celebration, and with more than a hundred ideas contained within these pages, there should be something for everyone. From simple geometric patterns commemorating a milestone anniversary to intricate studies stitched for someone special, we have tried to cover all levels of cross stitching experience. If you are a beginner, small projects such as greetings cards are the perfect way to practise your technique; if you are a more experienced stitcher, you could use these quick-to-stitch designs to try out some of the specialist threads and fabrics now available, such as the metallic thread used on page 101. In addition, using leftover threads and off-cuts of fabric from larger projects to make up greetings cards is both cheap and environmentally friendly.

Mounting your work using double-fold card blanks with ready-cut apertures is quick and easy and will give your stitching a professional finish. Single-fold card blanks allow you to provide extra decoration by pulling threads or fraying the edges of the background fabric. We have also included suggestions for a few more adventurous finishing touches, such as ribbon, glitter, confetti and even sandpaper to create a truly unique card, and have given instructions for making simple but stylish double mounts.

When you have stitched some of the complete designs, try using the selection of motifs and borders given at the end of each chapter to design your own cards. All you need are a few coloured pencils and some graph paper. Alternatively, you can enhance the decorative effect by adding matching motifs to your tablecloth, napkins and name cards. With a little imagination, you can incorporate attractive and appropriate cross stitch designs almost anywhere.

Cross stitch is similar to painting by numbers. Each square of fabric is allocated its colour individually, but as you stitch and the squares begin to work together, the picture is gradually revealed. As with painting, different design styles can be achieved. For example, by using the same thread in blocks of colour, flat, cartoon-like images can be formed, like the clown design on page

above: cards can be stitched to suit any occasion. Experiment with different mounting techniques to create your desired effect.

96; however, using different shades of the same colour can create an illusion of depth, giving the design a three-dimensional appearance, as with the Edwardian lady on page 85. Another way to give an extra dimension to your stitching is to add texture, which can be achieved by incorporating French knots, as shown in the giraffe design on page 91.

Using a coloured fabric can also make a big difference to the appearance of your finished picture. Thread colours that look fresh and clean when stitched on a white fabric can appear dull and muddy when worked on a darker fabric. This tendency can be corrected by increasing the number of strands used

when stitching, which will give better coverage and a more intense colour. By using a bold primary colour you can add a touch of fun and life to a simple motif, or you can increase the sophistication by using a subtle shade. The possibilities and variations are almost limitless, and stitching greetings cards is the perfect way to experiment – just in case the design doesn't quite work out as planned!

We hope that you will use the designs and ideas in this book both to celebrate those special moments with friends and relatives and as a springboard for your own creativity.

Happy stitching!

Births, Christenings and Special Birthdays

The arrival of a new member of the family and their first few birthdays are always special occasions, but remember that older friends and relatives have important birthdays too! Mark all these events with a beautiful keepsake card.

Bunny with bottle

Duck with bootee and rattle

Little girl's 1st birthday

Little boy's 1st birthday

Birthday cake

Party hats

Horoscopes

Woman's 70th birthday

Man's 70th birthday

Grandma's kitchen

Grandpa's garden

Motifs and borders

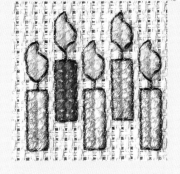

Bunny with bottle

Stitch this cute bunny as the perfect welcome for a new baby in your family.

Key

	DMC	Anchor		DMC	Anchor
+	blanc	1	×	739	366
T	318	399	−	762	397
■	413	236	▲	913	241
△	415	234			
●	603	55	**Backstitch**		
○	605	1094		DMC	Anchor
I	712	926	╲	413	236

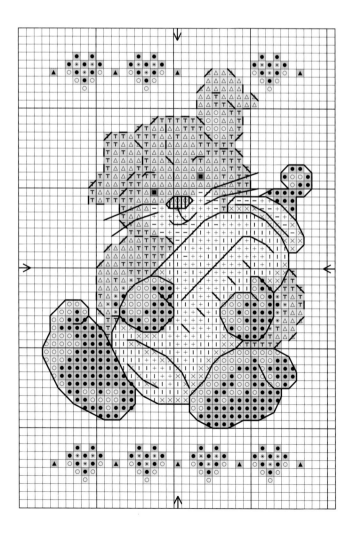

Measurements

The cross stitch design measures 10 x 7cm (4 x 2¾in)

Materials

- 15cm (6in) square of white 14-count Aida fabric
- One skein of stranded cotton in each colour listed in the key
- Size 26 tapestry needle
- Pink single-fold card blank measuring 10 x 14.5cm (4 x 5¾in)

Stitch details

Cross stitch use 2 strands
Backstitch use 1 strand

Note

When the stitching is complete, trim to six Aida blocks around the design. Fray two blocks and then stick on to the card.

Duck with bootee and rattle

There are three charming motifs for a baby in this card, which would be ideal for a friend's or relative's new arrival.

Key

	DMC	Anchor
O	744	301
+	747	158
I	3078	292
▲	3839	136
N	3840	144
×	3854	302

Backstitch

	DMC	Anchor
╲	792	139
╲	920	339

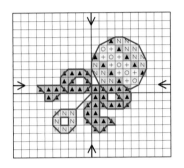

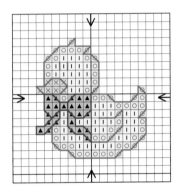

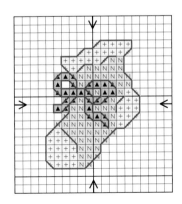

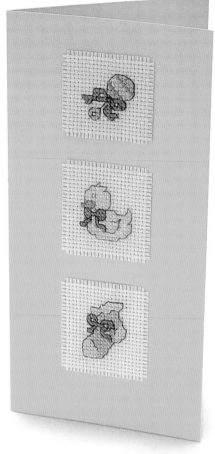

Measurements

Each cross stitch design measures 3cm (1¼in) square

Materials

- Three 10cm (4in) squares of white 14-count Aida fabric
- One skein of stranded cotton in each colour listed in the key
- Size 26 tapestry needle
- Yellow single-fold card blank measuring 10 x 20cm (4 x 8in)

Stitch details

Cross stitch use 2 strands
Backstitch use 1 strand

Note

When the stitching is complete, trim each motif to five Aida blocks around the design. Fray one block and then stick on to the card.

Little girl's 1st birthday

Mark the occasion of a girl's first birthday with a party, a present and a card so that you can treasure the memory.

Key

	DMC	Anchor			DMC	Anchor
+	blanc	1		✕	976	309
■	310	403		U	996	433
·	353	6				
▲	601	77		**Backstitch**		
Z	604	55			DMC	Anchor
T	666	46		◥	310	403
O	975	370				

Measurements

The cross stitch design measures 7.5 x 7cm (2⅞ x 2¾in)

Materials

- 13cm (5in) square of white 18-count Aida fabric
- One skein of stranded cotton in each colour listed in the key
- Size 26 tapestry needle
- Pink double-fold card blank measuring 10 x 10cm (4in) with a 9cm (3½in) square aperture

Stitch details

Cross stitch use 2 strands
Backstitch use 1 strand

Little boy's 1st birthday

Remember the first birthday, the first cake and the first candle to be blown out? Capture a magic moment that can never be revisited.

Key

	DMC	Anchor			DMC	Anchor
■	310	403		◉	975	370
·	353	6		▢	996	433
∎	666	46				
✕	702	226		**Backstitch**		
+	743	305			DMC	Anchor
−	797	132		◥	310	403
▲	823	150				

Measurements
The cross stitch design measures 7.5 x 7cm (2⅞ x 2¾in)

Materials
- 13cm (5in) square of white 18-count Aida fabric
- One skein of stranded cotton in each colour listed in the key
- Size 26 tapestry needle
- Blue double-fold card blank measuring 10 x 10cm (4 x 4in) with a 9cm (3½in) square aperture

Stitch details
Cross stitch use 2 strands
Backstitch use 1 strand

Birthday cake

Give someone special a birthday treat – a cake without calories! This card is suitable for a friend or relative of any age.

Measurements
The cross stitch design measures 11 x 4cm (4¼ x 1½in)

Materials
- 18cm (7in) square of white 14-count Aida fabric
- One skein of stranded cotton in each colour listed in the key
- Size 26 tapestry needle
- Bright pink single-fold card blank measuring 10 x 21cm (4 x 8¼in)

Stitch details
Cross stitch use 2 strands
Backstitch use 1 strand

Note
When the stitching is complete, trim to six Aida blocks around the design. Fray one block and then stick on to the card.

Key

	DMC	Anchor
−	blanc	1
●	326	39
O	436	363
×	604	23
U	738	361
+	742	302
▲	744	301
H	775	1037
I	818	49

Backstitch

	DMC	Anchor
＼	3834	972

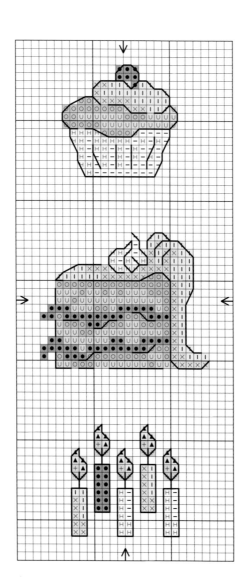

Party hats

Celebrate a loved one's birthday with these cheerful and brightly coloured party hats.

Measurements
The cross stitch design measures 7cm (2¾in) square

Materials
- 13cm (5in) square of pale lemon 14-count Aida fabric
- One skein of stranded cotton in each colour listed in the key
- Size 26 tapestry needle
- Turquoise double-fold card blank measuring 10.5 x 15cm (4⅛ x 6in) with an 8cm (3in) square aperture

Stitch details
Cross stitch use 2 strands
Backstitch use 1 strand

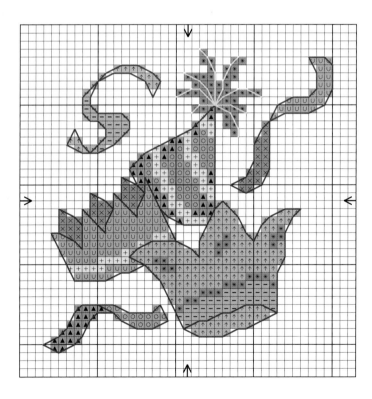

Key					
	DMC	**Anchor**		**DMC**	**Anchor**
+	307	290	−	3845	433
*	333	99			
▲	600	57	**Backstitch**		
O	602	55		**DMC**	**Anchor**
X	701	245	⟋	307	290
U	703	256	⟍	550	102
↑	3843	410			

Horoscopes

Choose the appropriate design from the 12 signs of the zodiac to make a personalized birthday card for the stargazer in your life.

Measurements
Each cross stitch design measures 6.5 x 5cm (2⅝ x 2in)

Materials
• 13cm (5in) square of 16-count Aida for each design in your chosen colour (shown: Scorpio – eau-de-Nil; Taurus – ice blue; Aquarius – Christmas red)
• One skein of stranded cotton in each colour listed in the key
• Size 26 tapestry needle
• Double-fold card blank measuring 10.5 x 15cm (4⅛ x 6in) with a 5.5 x 7cm (2¼ x 2¾in) rectangular aperture in your chosen colour (shown: Scorpio – green; Taurus – blue; Aquarius – red)

Stitch details
Cross stitch use 2 strands
Backstitch use 1 strand

Key	DMC	Anchor		DMC	Anchor
⊠	208	98	F	955	206
▽	209	96	O	3766	1062
★	211	103	I	3823	275
⋈	351	10	×	3825	313
▲	352	8	●	3839	136
S	353	6	I	3840	144
U	598	1060	=	3855	311
−	747	158			
+	775	128	**Backstitch**		
*	911	230		DMC	Anchor
△	913	209	╲	930	1036
•	930	1036			

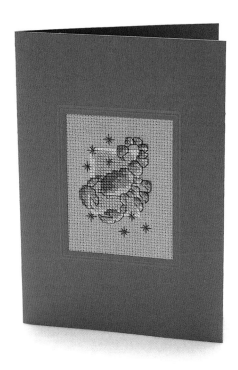

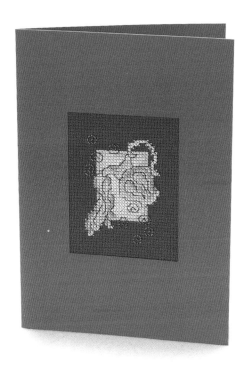

CAPRICORN

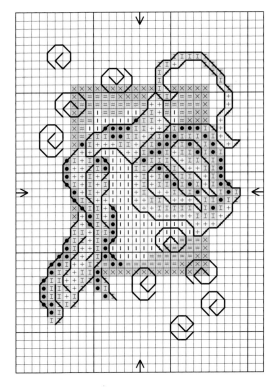

AQUARIUS

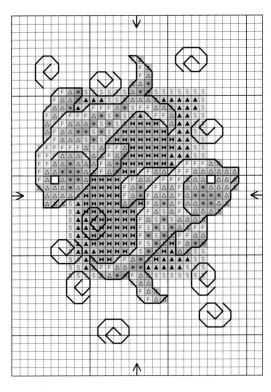

PISCES

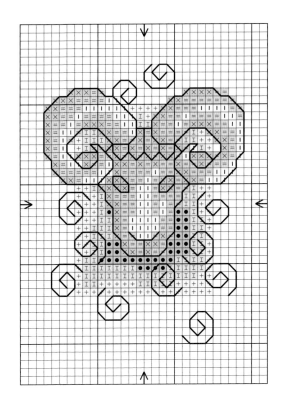

ARIES

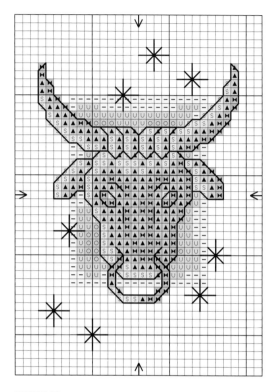

TAURUS

GEMINI

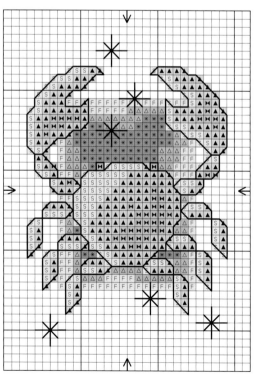

CANCER

LEO

VIRGO

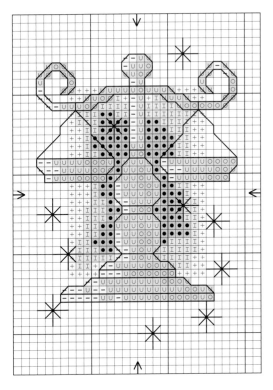

LIBRA

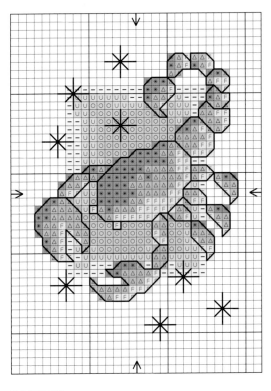

SCORPIO

SAGITTARIUS

Woman's 70th birthday

The mass of dainty violets tumbling out of this flower-filled basket makes this a spectacular card. Choose it to send to a friend or relative to mark a retirement or birthday.

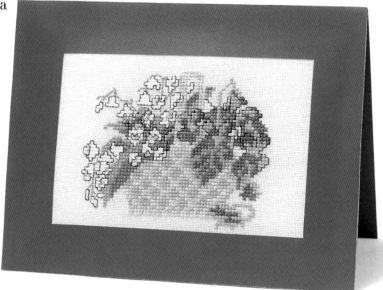

Measurements

The cross stitch design measures 8.5 x 11cm (3¼ x 4¼in)

Materials

- 14.5 x 20cm (5¾ x 8in) of white 28-count evenweave fabric
- One skein of stranded cotton in each colour listed in the key
- Size 26 tapestry needle
- Purple double-fold card blank measuring 20 x 14.5cm (8 x 5¾in) with a 9.5 x 14.5cm (3¾ x 5¾in) rectangular aperture

Stitch details

Work each stitch over 2 fabric threads
Cross stitch use 2 strands
Backstitch use 1 strand

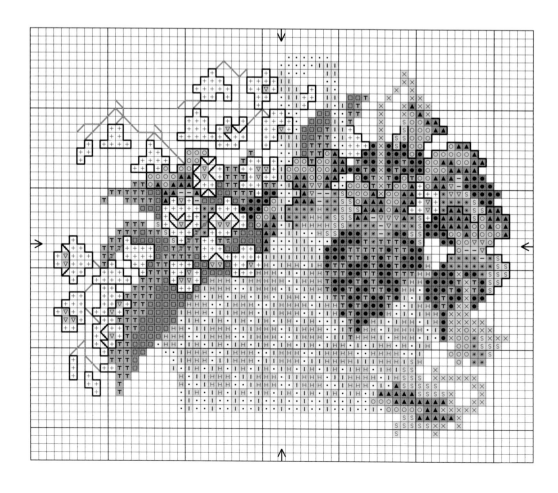

Key

	DMC	Anchor
+	blanc	1
■	341	117
S	580	924
●	613	853
H	676	891
I	677	300
·	733	280
T	831	277
☐	833	907
Z	972	298
▽	973	290
−	3047	886
O	3348	264
X	3740	872
▲	3746	118

Backstitch

	DMC	Anchor
✳	310	403
╲	733	280

Man's 70th birthday

This card will trigger memories of an older friend's or relative's favourite pastimes. Change the numbers in the top right-hand corner to match the recipient's age.

Measurements

The cross stitch design measures 6 x 7.5cm (2½ x 2⅞in)

Materials

- 13cm (5in) square of white 18-count Aida fabric
- One skein of stranded cotton in each colour listed in the key
- Size 26 tapestry needle
- Bright green double-fold card blank measuring 13 x 13cm (5 x 5in) with an 8cm (3in) square aperture

Stitch details

Cross stitch use 1 strands
Backstitch use 1 strand

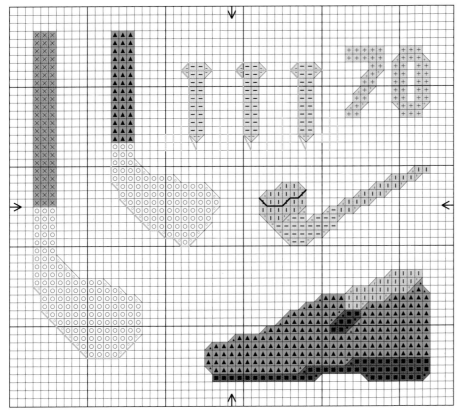

Key

	DMC	Anchor
▲	301	349
■	310	403
−	738	361
✕	781	309
I	927	849
+	954	225
O	3072	847

Backstitch

	DMC	Anchor
◥	310	403
◥	927	849
◥	954	225

Grandma's kitchen

Show your appreciation for grandma's nurturing role in your life by stitching her this jolly card to celebrate her birthday.

Measurements

The cross stitch design measures 9cm (3½in) square

Materials

- 20cm (8in) square of cream 14-count Aida fabric
- One skein of stranded cotton in each colour listed in the key
- Size 26 tapestry needle
- Bright pink double-fold card blank measuring 14.5 x 20cm (5¾ x 8in) with a 9.5 x 12cm (3¾ x 4½in) rectangular aperture

Stitch details

Cross stitch use 2 strands
Backstitch use 1 strand

Key

	DMC	Anchor
·	blanc	1
■	154	72
X	318	399
▼	356	1013
S	415	234
O	436	363
H	725	291
I	727	289
+	951	1011
–	3609	85
Z	3806	55
✗	3829	369
T	3859	1007

Backstitch

	DMC	Anchor
＼	154	72
＼	304	13
＼	725	291
＼	3806	55

Grandpa's garden

If your grandpa enjoys growing beautiful flowers in the garden or an allotment, stitch this special card to help him mark his birthday.

Measurements
The cross stitch design measures 9cm (3½in) square

Materials
- 20cm (8in) square of cream 14-count Aida fabric
- One skein of stranded cotton in each colour listed in the key
- Size 26 tapestry needle
- Lavender double-fold card blank measureing 14.5 x 20cm (5¾ x 8in) with a 9.5 x 12cm (3¾ x 4½in) rectangular aperture

Stitch details
Cross stitch use 2 strands
Backstitch use 1 strand

Key

	DMC	Anchor
·	blanc	1
■	154	72
X	318	399
✓	341	121
▼	356	1013
S	415	234
H	725	291
I	727	289
⊡	793	939
N	912	241
+	951	1011
−	3609	85
Z	3806	55
T	3859	895

Backstitch

	DMC	Anchor
╲	154	72
╲	304	13
╲	725	291
╲	909	923

Motifs and borders

Incorporate some of these motifs into the designs in this section to personalize your cards. The rocking-horses and rattles would be delightful additions to a card for a newborn baby, while the cakes and balloons would be colourful additions to a birthday card. You could even add the appropriate number of candles.

Key

	DMC	Anchor			DMC	Anchor
I	blanc	1		−	955	206
●	413	236		N	972	298
Z	436	363		S	3078	292
■	601	29				
T	603	55		**Backstitch**		
I	605	1094			DMC	Anchor
X	726	295		╲	413	236
▼	798	131		╲	601	29
∩	800	128		╲	798	131
O	809	120		╲	910	228
▣	910	228		╲	913	203
△	913	203		╲	972	298

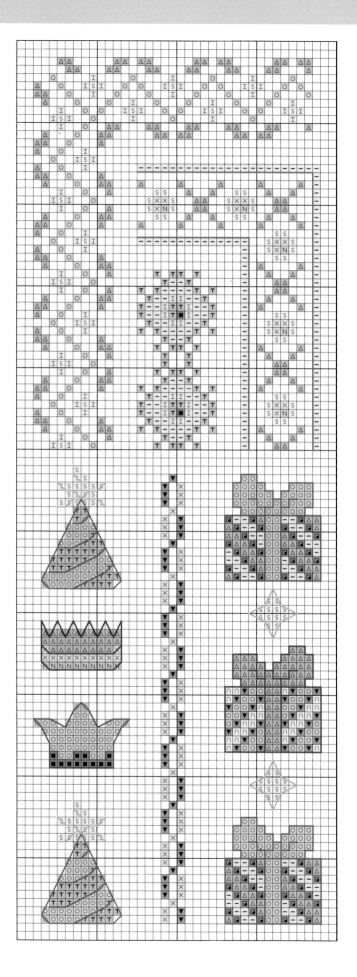

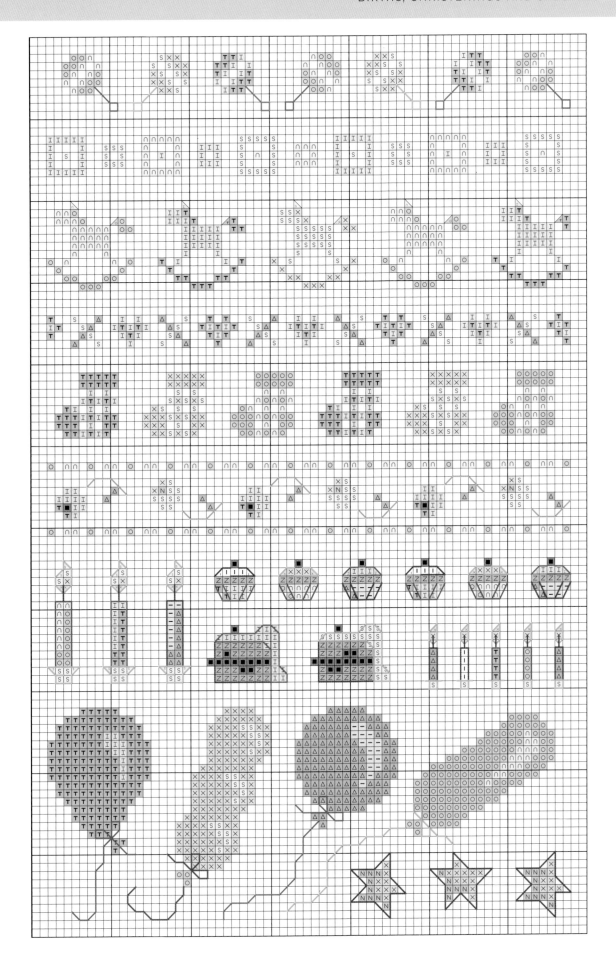

Special Occasions

Whether it's a wedding, anniversary or exam success, every special event deserves to be celebrated. These delightful designs will help you to do so in style!

Wedding congratulations

Wedding cake

Bridesmaids

From this day forward

Silver wedding anniversary

Golden wedding anniversary

Good luck

New home

Driving test

Moving abroad or travel

Get well soon

Graduation celebrations

Motifs and borders

Wedding congratulations

Getting married is an important step and represents a major life change. Let the happy couple know how pleased you are for them on their big day.

Measurements
The cross stitch design measures 6.5 x 5cm (2⅝ x 2in)

Materials
- 13cm (5in) square of white 18-count Aida fabric
- One skein of stranded cotton in each colour listed in the key
- Size 26 tapestry needle
- White double-fold card blank measuring 10.5 x 12.5cm (4 x 5in) with a 5.5 x 7.5cm (2¼ x 2⅞in) rectangular aperture

Stitch details
Cross stitch use 1 strand
Backstitch use 1 strand
French knots use 1 strand

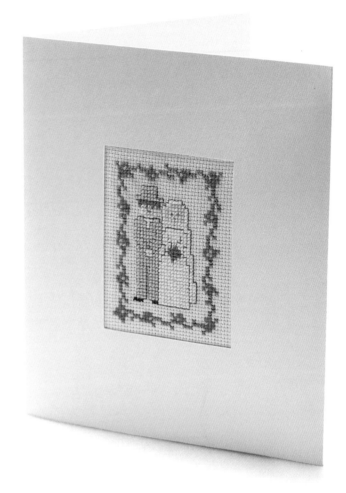

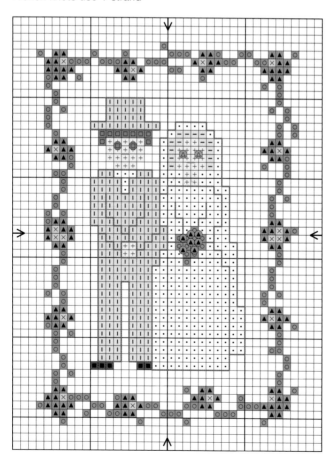

Key

	DMC	Anchor
·	blanc	1
▲	309	39
■	310	403
∪	317	400
I	415	398
▢	433	371
○	701	227
–	726	297
△	798	131
+	951	1011
✕	3341	328

Backstitch

	DMC	Anchor
╲	317	400

French knots

	DMC	Anchor
▲	309	39
▢	433	371
△	798	131

Wedding cake

Show the bride- and groom-to-be how much you care by stitching this pretty, rose-covered cake, which looks good enough to eat but will keep forever.

Measurements

The cross stitch design measures 7cm (2¾in) square

Materials

- 15cm (6in) square of white 14-count Aida fabric
- One skein of stranded cotton in each colour listed in the key
- Size 26 tapestry needle
- Pale pink double-fold card blank measuring 14.5cm (5¾in) square with a 9.5cm (3¾in) square aperture
- 13cm (5in) square of bright pink card

Stitch details

Cross stitch use 2 strands
Backstitch use 1 strand
French knots use 3 strands

Note

Cut an aperture in the square of bright pink card so that it is slightly smaller than the one in the card blank. Stick it to the inside of the card blank to create a stylish double-mount effect. Then mount the finished stitching in the usual way.

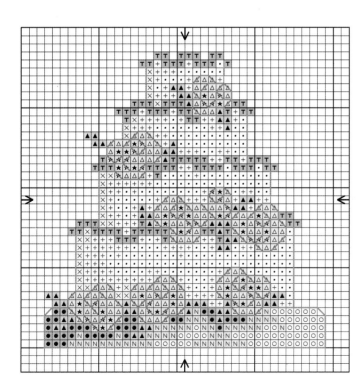

Key

	DMC	Anchor
·	blanc	1
●	414	399
N	415	234
O	762	2
△	818	49
▲	993	206
★	3716	23
×	3753	1031
+	3756	1037

Backstitch

	DMC	Anchor
◥	414	399
◥	3831	63

French knots

	DMC	Anchor
T	956	54

Bridesmaids

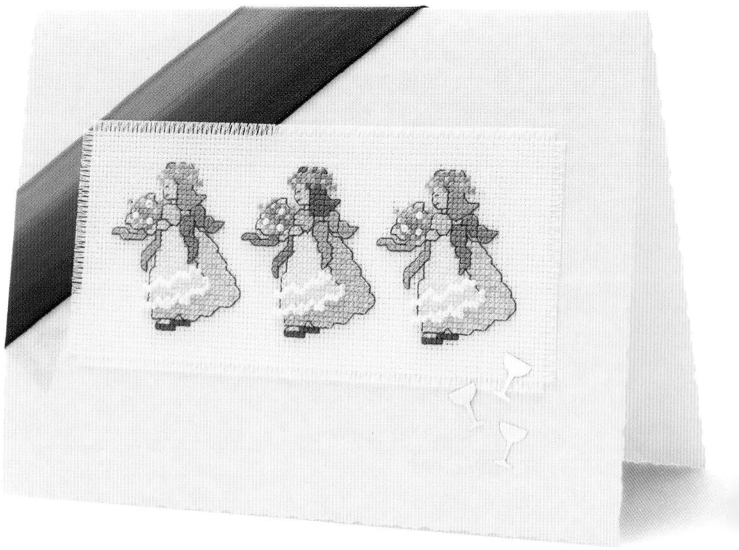

These three little bridesmaids all in a row are the perfect escort to accompany a bride down the aisle on her special day.

Measurements

The cross stitch design measures 5.5 x 14cm (2¼ x 5½in)

Materials

- 20cm (8in) square of white 16-count Aida fabric
- One skein of stranded cotton in each colour listed in the key
- Size 26 tapestry needle
- Pale pink single-fold card blank measuring 15 x 20cm (6 x 8in)
- Purple ribbon
- Champagne-glass confetti
- White seed beads

Stitch details

Cross stitch use 2 strands

Backstitch use 1 strand

Beading use 1 strand to attach the beads

Note

When the stitching is complete, trim to eight Aida blocks around the design and fray one block. Stick a length of purple ribbon across the corner of the card with double-sided tape, then mount the stitching on top in the usual way. Finally, carefully glue on some champagne-glass confetti for a really personal touch.

Key

	DMC	Anchor
+	blanc	1
□	164	240
▽	210	96
−	211	103
▲	437	1008
U	744	301
I	818	48
●	840	1084
N	842	1080
×	966	1043
○	3716	23
■	3740	1019
↑	3770	1011

Backstitch

	DMC	Anchor
╲	3740	1019

Beading

✳ white seed beads

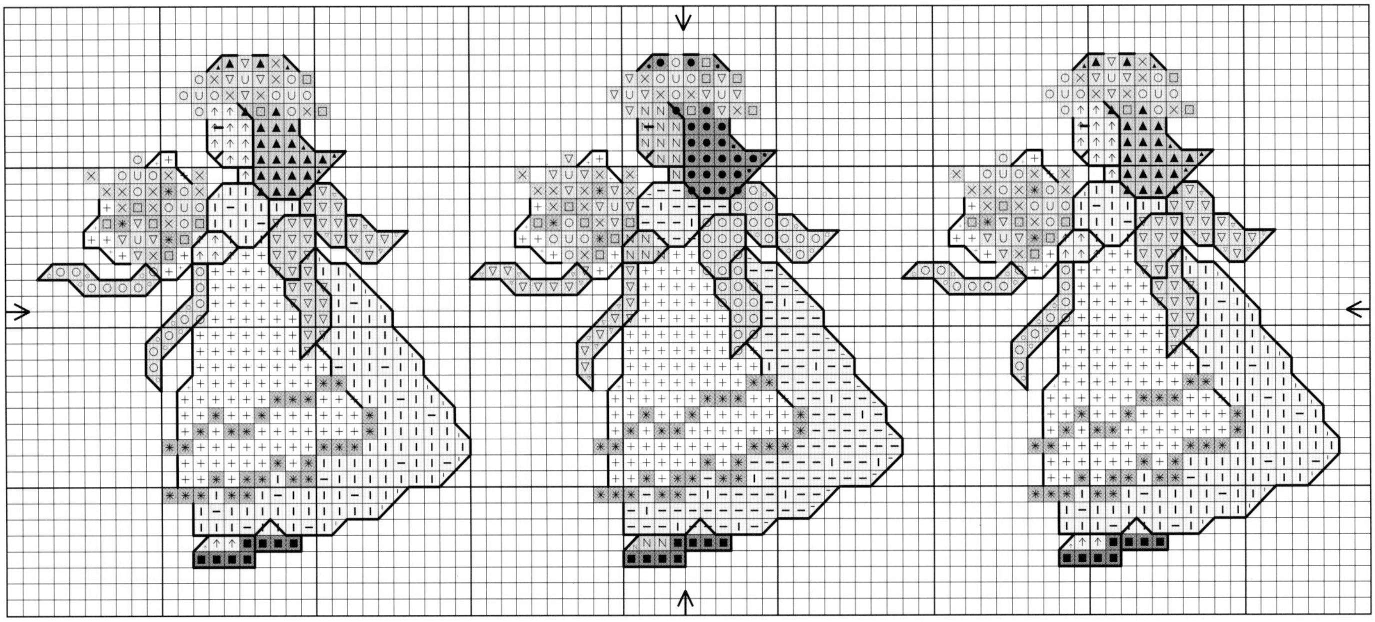

From this day forward

Celebrate a marriage with this happy explosion of stylish wedding-day motifs.

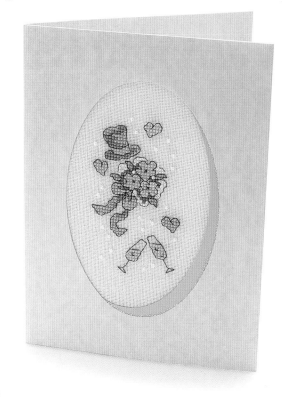

Measurements
The cross stitch design measures 10 x 7cm (4 x 2¾in)

Materials
- 20cm (8in) square of white 28-count Zweigart Brittney evenweave fabric
- One skein of stranded cotton in each colour listed in the key
- Size 26 tapestry needle
- One pale green and one metallic grey double-fold card blank, each measuring 15 x 20cm (6 x 8in) with a 9.5 x 14.5cm (3¾ x 5¾in) oval aperture
- Glitter glue
- White seed beads

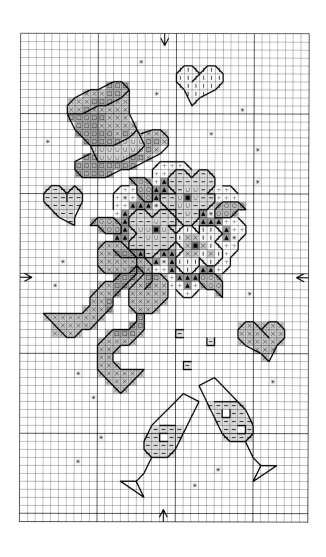

Stitch details
Work each stitch over 2 fabric threads
Cross stitch use 2 strands
Backstitch use 1 strand
Beading use 1 strand to attach the beads

Note
Trim the grey card blank and stick it behind the green card, slightly off centre, then highlight the edge with glitter glue. Mount the finished stitching in the usual way.

Key					
	DMC	**Anchor**		**DMC**	**Anchor**
+	blanc	1	U	3824	8
×	159	1033			
□	160	1034	**Backstitch**		
▲	163	876		**DMC**	**Anchor**
○	563	203	◺	930	1035
I	775	1037			
■	930	1035	**Beading**		
–	945	1012	✳	white seed beads	

Silver wedding anniversary

Twenty-five years together is cause for celebration. Metallic thread is used for this simple design, which will commemorate a very special day.

Measurements

The cross stitch design measures 6cm (2⅜in) square

Materials

- 15cm (6in) square of navy 14-count Aida fabric
- One skein of stranded cotton in each colour listed in the key
- Size 26 tapestry needle
- Metallic silver single-fold card measuring 10 x 15cm (4 x 6in)

Stitch details

Cross stitch use 2 strands
Backstitch use 2 strands

Note

When the stitching is complete, trim to six Aida blocks around the design. Fray two blocks and then stick on to the card.

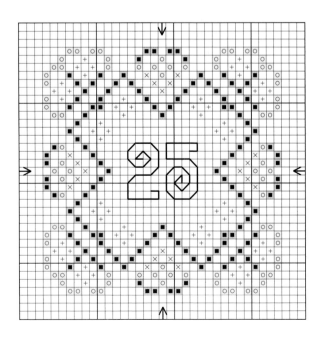

Key

	DMC	Anchor	Backstitch		
■	3839	121		**DMC**	**Anchor**
○	3840	120	╲	5283	00301
✕	3841	128			
+	5283	00301			

Golden wedding anniversary

If you enjoy fine needlework, this design looks pretty worked in miniature, but it is equally effective worked on a lower count fabric.

Measurements
The cross stitch design measures 3.5cm (1⅜in) square

Materials
- 10cm (4in) square of cream 22-count Hardanger fabric
- One skein of stranded cotton in each colour listed in the key
- Size 26 tapestry needle
- Pale blue single-fold card blank measuring 9 x 11.5cm (3½ x 4⅝in) with a heart-shaped aperture

Stitch details
Work each stitch over 1 pair of fabric threads
Cross stitch use 1 strand
Backstitch use 1 strand

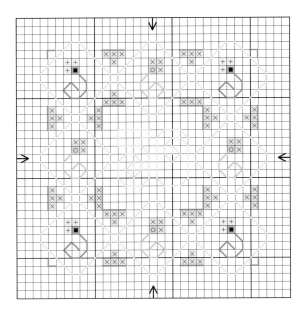

Key

	DMC	Anchor	Backstitch	DMC	Anchor
○	368	260			
■	992	1072	◺	368	260
✕	3840	128	◺	992	1072
+	5282	00300	◺	5282	00300

Good luck

Wish someone all the best with this collection of lucky charms. The beautiful black feline makes it particularly suitable to give to a cat lover.

Key

	DMC	Anchor
■	310	403
I	318	234
◎	703	256
−	754	49
+	762	2
✕	3799	400

Backstitch

	DMC	Anchor
☐	762	2
◥	991	217
◥	3799	400

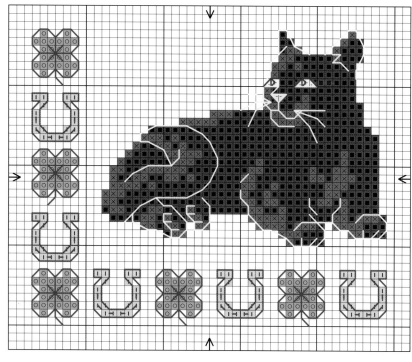

Measurements

The cross stitch design measures 7 x 9cm (2¾ x 3½in)

Materials

- 18cm (7in) square of ice-blue 14-count Aida fabric
- One skein of stranded cotton in each colour listed in the key
- Size 26 tapestry needle
- Green double-fold card blank measuring 11.5 x 18cm (4⅜ x 7in) with a 7.5 x 11cm (2⅞ x 4¼in) rectangular aperture

Stitch details

Cross stitch use 2 strands
Backstitch use 1 strand

New home

Moving house is one of the biggest, most expensive and longest thought-about decisions we make. It is certainly not an event that should pass unnoticed.

Measurements

The cross stitch design measures 12.5 x 7.5cm (4¾ x 2⅞in)

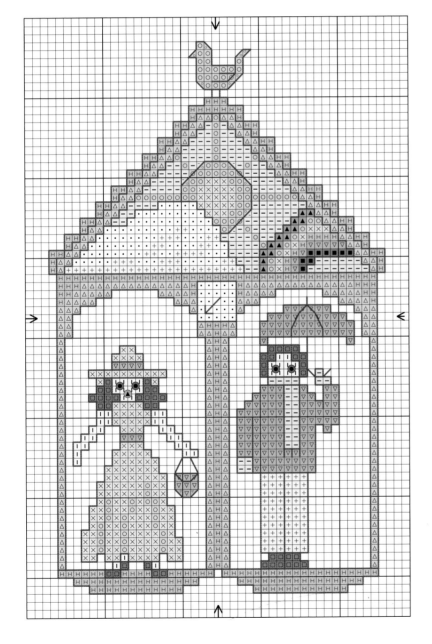

Materials

- 14.5 x 20cm (5¾ x 8in) of white 14-count Aida fabric
- One skein of stranded cotton in each colour listed in the key
- Size 26 tapestry needle
- Pale green double-fold card blank measuring 12 x 17cm (4¾ x 6¾in) with a 9.5 x 14.5cm (3¾ x 5¾in) rectangular aperture

Stitch details

Cross stitch use 2 strands
Backstitch use 1 strand
French knots use 1 strand

Key

	DMC	Anchor		DMC	Anchor
·	blanc	1	▽	3755	140
▲	321	9046			
■	550	101	**Backstitch**		
H	563	208		DMC	Anchor
△	564	206	◣	3799	400
O	742	302			
×	744	301	**French knots**		
▣	801	358		DMC	Anchor
I	819	271	▲	321	9046
—	828	158	●	3799	236
+	3072	397			

Driving test

You have cause for celebration if you have just passed your driving test. This is definitely a card for a careful driver. Does anyone you know deserve one?

Key

	DMC	Anchor			DMC	Anchor
·	blanc	1		–	3032	832
■	310	403		●	3362	263
○	318	399		▢	3363	262
×	522	860				
I	524	858		**Backstitch**		
▲	640	393			DMC	Anchor
+	783	306		◣	310	403

Measurements

The cross stitch design measures 8 x 13cm (3 x 5in)

Materials

• 14.5 x 20cm (5¾ x 8in) of white 14-count Aida fabric
• One skein of stranded cotton in each colour listed in the key
• Size 26 tapestry needle

• Dark green double-fold card blank measuring 12 x 17cm (4¾ x 6¾in) with a 9.5 x 14.5cm (3¾ x 5¾in) rectangular aperture

Stitch details

Cross stitch use 2 strands
Backstitch use 1 strand

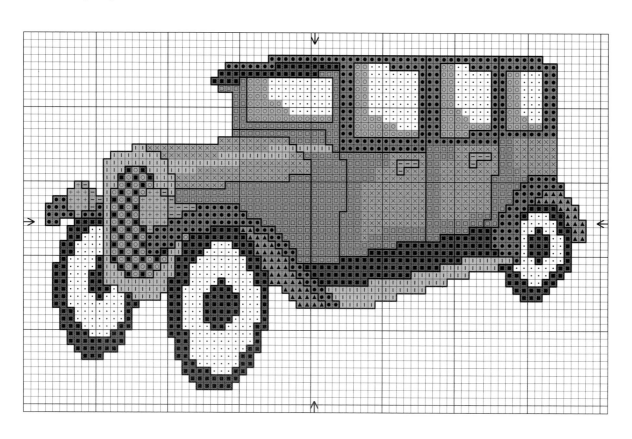

Moving abroad or travel

If a friend is planning to move abroad or take an extended trek in a distant country, this card will be the perfect way to wish them bon voyage.

Measurements

The cross stitch design measures 7.5 x 5cm (2⅞ x 2in)

Materials

- 13cm (5in) square of white 18-count Aida fabric
- One skein of stranded cotton in each colour listed in the key
- Size 26 tapestry needle
- Blue double-fold card blank measuring 10.5 x 13.5cm (4 x 5¼in) with a 5.5 x 8.5cm (2¼ x 3¼in) rectangular aperture

Stitch details

Cross stitch use 1 strand
Backstitch use 1 strand
French knots use 1 strand

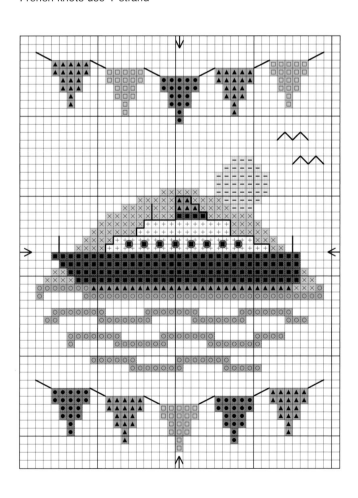

Key					
	DMC	**Anchor**	**Backstitch**		
+	blanc	1		**DMC**	**Anchor**
■	310	403	◥	310	403
✕	519	167			
▲	666	46	**French knots**		
−	726	295		**DMC**	**Anchor**
□	740	316	■	310	403
●	797	132			
○	958	187			

Get well soon

Flowers are always appreciated and cheering. Why not give this pretty design to someone you know who is feeling a little under the weather?

Measurements

The cross stitch design measures 4.5 x 6.5cm (1¾ x 2⅝in)

Materials

- 13cm (5in) square of white 18-count Aida fabric
- One skein of stranded cotton in each colour listed in the key
- Size 26 tapestry needle
- Red double-fold card blank measuring 12.5 x 14.5cm (5 x 5¾in) with a 7 x 9cm (2¾ x 3½in) rectangular aperture

Stitch details

Cross stitch use 1 strand
Backstitch use 1 strand

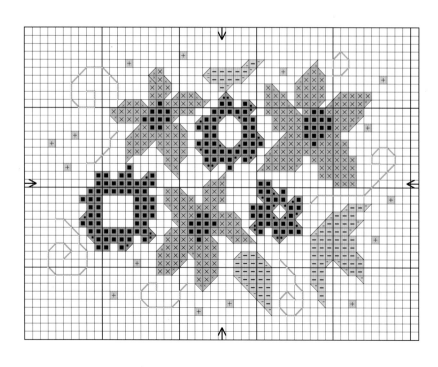

Key		
	DMC	**Anchor**
−	977	313
+	3042	870
■	3726	970
✕	3778	9575
Backstitch		
	DMC	**Anchor**
╲	3042	870

Graduation celebrations

Congratulate the scholar in your family on their great achievement with this quirky graduation card.

Key

	DMC	Anchor			DMC	Anchor
■	310	403		▲	3799	400
·	712	2				
−	739	892		**Backstitch**		
I	743	311			DMC	Anchor
✕	950	4146		◣	310	403
○	996	1090		□	712	2
▣	3772	1007		◥	3772	1007

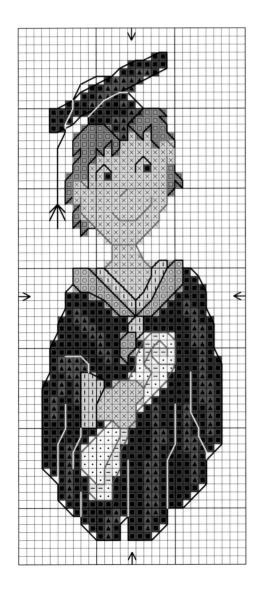

Measurements
The cross stitch design measures 4.5 x 11.5cm (1¾ x 4⅜in)

Materials
- 20cm (8in) square of white 14-count Aida fabric
- One skein of stranded cotton in each colour listed in the key
- Size 26 tapestry needle
- White double-fold card blank measuring 20 x 15cm (8 x 6in) with a 9.5 x 13.5cm (3¾ x 5¼in) oval aperture

Stitch details
Cross stitch use 2 strands
Backstitch use 1 strand

Motifs and borders

Give cards designed to celebrate a special occasion an extra special touch. Top hats and champagne glasses are the perfect motifs for cards bearing wedding congratulations, and even people who claim not to be superstitious will appreciate some four-leaved clovers or horseshoes if they are about to sit an exam or take a driving test.

Key

	DMC	Anchor		DMC	Anchor
⊡	317	235	−	989	265
O	318	398	▼	991	217
✗	333	99	U	3716	23
I	340	108	→	3747	128
●	355	1014	■	3799	400
T	356	1013			
4	554	103	**Backstitch**		
Z	562	209		DMC	Anchor
S	676	361	◣	340	108
·	712	2	◣	355	1014
✕	743	311	◣	562	209
+	745	386	◣	989	265
↑	818	271	◣	991	217
N	961	40	◣	3716	23
◪	988	266	◣	3799	400

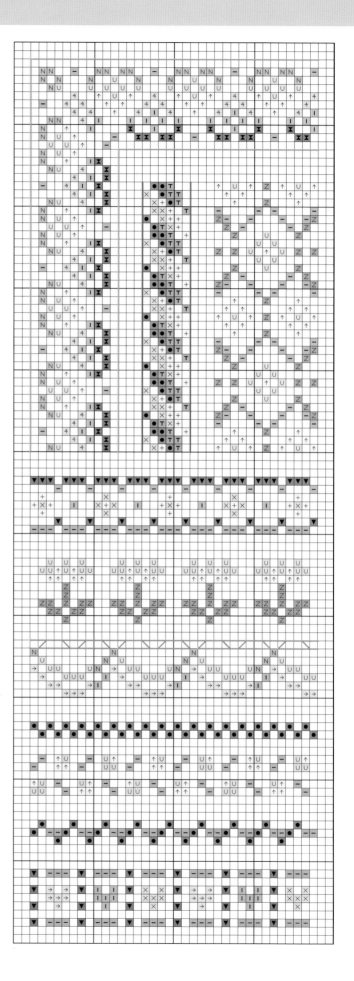

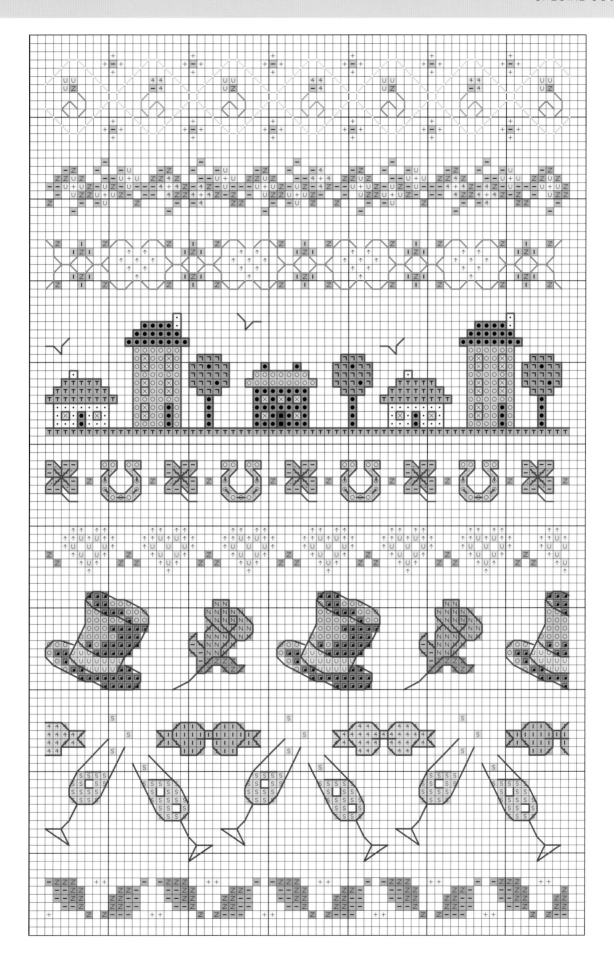

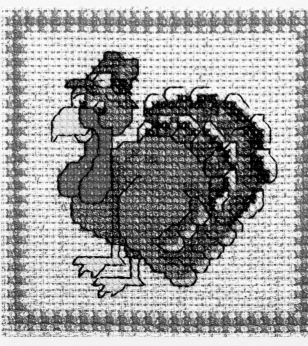

Celebrations

Greetings cards are often discarded once the occasion for which they were intended has passed, but you can be certain that your hand-stitched card will be kept as a treasured souvenir of a special date.

Santa

If you are looking for a challenging and fairly substantial project, try stitching Santa. He would make a perfect card, or you could frame him as a keepsake that can be brought out each year.

Key

	DMC	Anchor			DMC	Anchor
·	blanc	1		▲	797	132
●	304	47		○	970	324
■	310	403		＊	975	370
✕	318	399		I	976	309
▫	353	6				
▽	666	46		**Backstitch**		
−	701	227			DMC	Anchor
S	741	314		＼	975	370
＋	762	234				

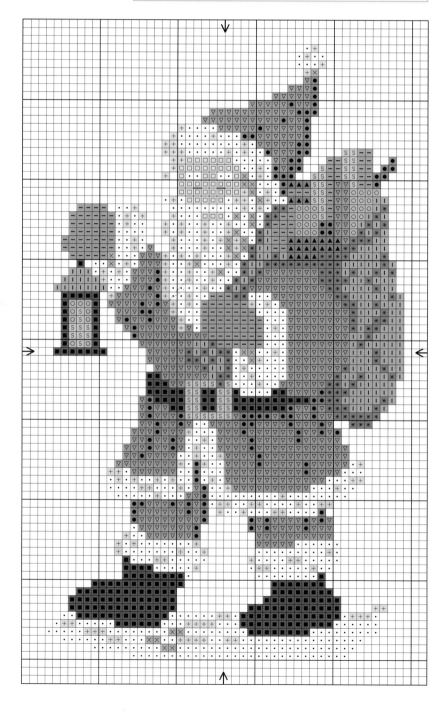

Measurements

The cross stitch design measures 13 x 8.5cm (5 x 3¼in)

Materials

- 20 x 14.5cm (8 x 5¾in) of white 14-count Aida fabric
- One skein of stranded cotton in each colour listed in the key
- Size 26 tapestry needle
- Red double-fold card blank measuring 16 x 20cm (6¼ x 8in) with an 11 x 15cm (4¼ x 6in) rectangular aperture

Stitch details

Cross stitch use 2 strands
Backstitch use 1 strand

Christmas geese

Pass on your yuletide cheer with this seasonal card, depicting a trio of plump geese adorned with a Christmas wreath and ribbons.

Measurements
The cross stitch design measures 5.5 x 14cm (2¼ x 5½in)

Materials
- 20.5cm (8⅛in) square of navy 14-count Aida fabric
- One skein of stranded cotton in each colour listed in the key
- Size 26 tapestry needle
- Holly green single-fold card blank measuring 15.5 x 24cm (6¼ x 9½in)
- Christmas ribbon

Stitch details
Cross stitch use 2 strands
Backstitch use 1 strand
Three-quarter stitch use 2 strands
Quarter stitch use 2 strands

Note
When the stitching is complete, trim to eight Aida blocks around the design and fray two blocks. Stick a length of Christmas ribbon across the card with double-sided tape to add extra sparkle. Mount the stitching on top in the usual way.

Key

	DMC	Anchor	Backstitch		
				DMC	Anchor
+	blanc	1			
▲	666	46	◣	666	46
○	701	245	◣	701	245
–	722	324	◣	823	152
■	823	152			
✕	992	1072			
I	3072	926			

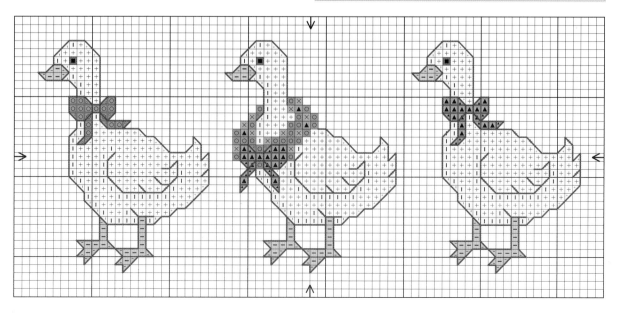

Snowman and reindeer

Brighten up the festivities by stitching this happy Christmas scene. A cheerful reindeer greets a jolly snowman, who is on his way home with his Christmas tree.

Measurements

The cross stitch design measures 7.5 x 12cm (2⅞ x 4½in)

Materials

- 20cm (8in) square of baby blue 14-count Aida fabric
- One skein of stranded cotton in each colour listed in the key
- Size 26 tapestry needle
- Dark metallic blue single-fold card blank measuring 15 x 20cm (6 x 8in)
- Gold stars

Stitch details

Cross stitch use 2 strands
Backstitch use 1 strand

Note

When the stitching is complete, trim to eight Aida blocks around the design. Fray two blocks and then stick on to the card. Then add some gold stars for extra Christmas cheer.

Key

	DMC	Anchor
+	blanc	1
✗	349	46
–	351	8
T	436	363
✕	738	361
▽	742	298
▲	911	230
○	913	203
●	3750	149
✳	3752	1031
I	3756	1037

Backstitch

	DMC	Anchor
╲	742	298
╲	902	22
╲	3750	149

Christmas kittens

These adorable kittens, with their very own Santa hat and stocking, make ideal cards to send to your favourite cat lovers at Christmas.

Measurements
The cross stitch designs measure 7.5cm (2⅞in) square and 5.5 x 6.5cm (2¼ x 2⅝in)

Materials
• Two 15cm (6in) squares of navy 14-count Aida fabric
• One skein of stranded cotton in each colour listed in the key
• Size 26 tapestry needle
• Two white single-fold card blanks, one measuring 14.5cm (5¾in) square and the other 15 x 20cm (6 x 8in)

Stitch details
Cross stitch use 2 strands
Backstitch use 2 strands

Note
When the stitching is complete, trim to eight Aida blocks around the design. Fray two blocks and then stick on to the card. Stitching one of the borders from page 56–7 would add some extra seasonal charm.

Key					
	DMC	Anchor		DMC	Anchor
·	blanc	1	+	3756	2
●	321	47	■	3799	400
I	414	235	▲	3801	46
×	415	234			
T	701	227	**Backstitch**		
○	704	255		DMC	Anchor
□	967	6	◣	3799	400
–	3706	35			

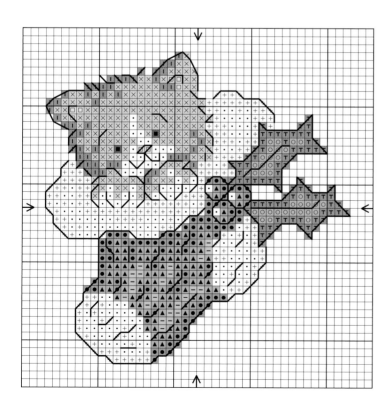
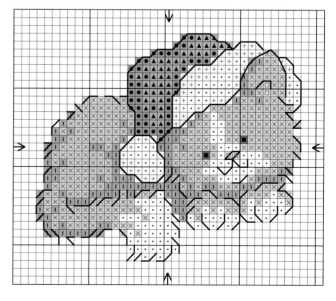

Happy New Year

See the New Year in with a celebration drink and look forward to the promising times ahead.

Measurements

The cross stitch design measures 7.5 x 5cm (2⅞ x 2in)

Materials

- 13cm (5in) square of white 18-count Aida fabric
- One skein of stranded cotton in each colour listed in the key
- Size 26 tapestry needle
- Blue double-fold card blank measuring 11 x 13cm (4¼ x 5in) with a 6 x 8cm (2½ x 3in) rectangular aperture

Stitch details

Cross stitch use 1 strand

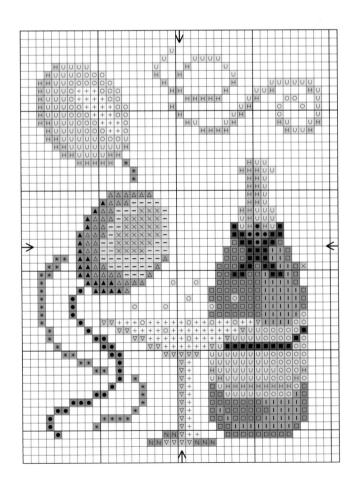

Key

	DMC	Anchor			DMC	Anchor
✕	209	109		＋	677	300
■	310	403		H	783	307
▲	327	100		●	815	22
△	553	98		✳	3765	169
—	554	97		I	3812	189
N	646	8581		□	3818	246
▽	648	900		U	3820	874
○	676	891				

Thanksgiving turkey

This jolly pilgrim turkey will bring a touch of humour to your Thanksgiving celebrations. The chunky check border complements the picture perfectly.

Measurements
The cross stitch design measures 9cm (3½in) square

Materials
- 20cm (8in) square of Rustico 14-count Aida fabric
- One skein of stranded cotton in each colour listed in the key
- Size 26 tapestry needle
- Bright red single-fold card blank measuring 14.5cm (5¾in) square

Stitch details
Cross stitch use 2 strands
Backstitch use 1 strand

Note
When the stitching is complete, trim to four Aida blocks around the design. Fray two blocks and then stick on to the card.

Key

	DMC	Anchor
+	blanc	1
■	310	403
●	349	334
U	351	328
▣	413	236
T	414	235
I	415	234
−	743	311
O	840	1084

Backstitch

	DMC	Anchor
╲	310	403

Easter chick

Sitting happily on a nest of colourful eggs, this cute little chick is the perfect way to convey your Easter greetings.

Measurements
The cross stitch design measures 7cm (2¾in) square

Materials
- 15cm (6in) square of white 14-count Aida fabric
- One skein of stranded cotton in each colour listed in the key
- Size 26 tapestry needle
- Pale green double-fold card blank measuring 14.5cm (5¾in) square with a 9.5cm (3¾in) square aperture
- 13cm (5in) square of baby blue card

Stitch details
Cross stitch use 2 strands
Backstitch use 1 strand

Note
Cut an aperture in the square of baby blue card so that it is slightly smaller than the one in the card blank. Stick it to the inside of the card to create a stylish double-mount effect. Then mount the finished stitching in the usual way.

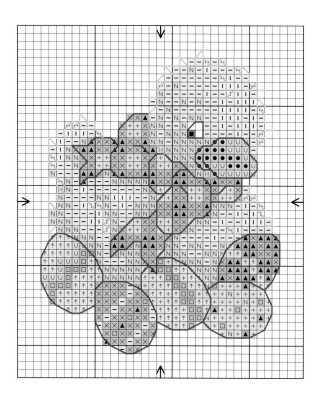

Key					
	DMC	Anchor		DMC	Anchor
⊡	340	108	↑	3747	128
■	413	236	●	3854	313
▲	597	1070	U	3855	314
N	726	298			
−	727	295	**Backstitch**		
+	955	1043		DMC	Anchor
×	959	185	◨	402	326
I	3078	292	◩	413	236

Easter bunny

Bring a smile to a loved one's face this spring by
stitching this cheerful bunny, which is carrying a
basket of Easter eggs.

Measurements
The cross stitch design measures 6.5 x 7cm (2⅝ x 2¾in)

Materials
• 15cm (6in) square of white 14-count Aida fabric
• One skein of stranded cotton in each colour listed in the key
• Size 26 tapestry needle
• Pale pink double-fold card blank measuring 15 x 20.5cm
  (6 x 8in) with a 10cm (4in) square aperture
• 13cm (5in) square of purple card

Stitch details
Cross stitch use 2 strands
Backstitch use 1 strand

Note
To add extra interest to the card, cut an aperture in the square of
purple card so that it is slightly smaller than the one in the card
blank. Stick it to the inside of the card to create a stylish double-
mount effect. Mount the finished stitching in the usual way.

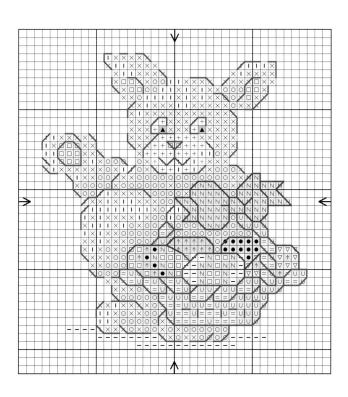

Key

	DMC	Anchor			DMC	Anchor
+	blanc	1	●		957	26
↑	209	97	□		963	23
O	318	235	▽		3761	928
▲	413	236	N		3766	168
×	415	234				
U	676	942	**Backstitch**			
=	677	300			DMC	Anchor
−	747	1037	◣		413	236
I	762	2	◣		930	1035

Hanukkah

Celebrate the festival of lights with this richly coloured Hanukkah card.

Measurements
The cross stitch design measures 8cm (3in) square

Materials
- 15cm (6in) square of white 16-count Aida fabric
- One skein of stranded cotton in each colour listed in the key
- Size 26 tapestry needle
- Dark green double-fold card blank measuring 14.5cm (5¾in) square with a 9.5cm (3¾in) square aperture

Stitch details
Cross stitch use 2 strands
Backstitch use 1 strand

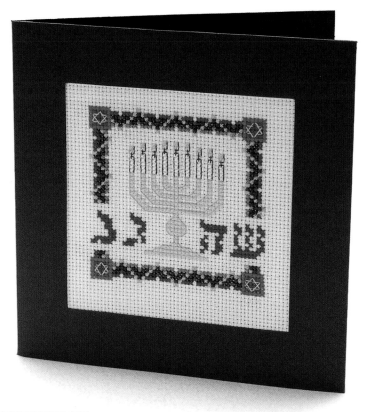

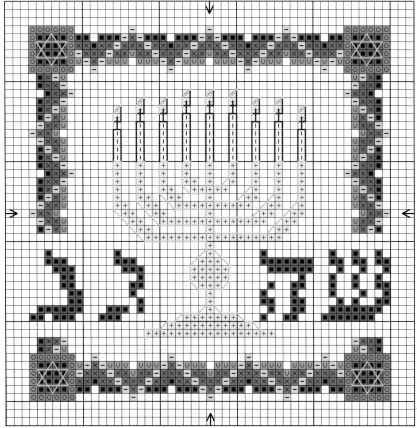

Key

	DMC	Anchor
I	blanc	1
■	777	43
✕	991	212
U	992	210
−	3820	306
+	3822	311
O	3831	41

Backstitch

	DMC	Anchor
╲	844	1041
╱	3820	306

Halloween

Spook all your friends on Halloween with this
cheerful pumpkin Jack-o'-lantern.

Key

	DMC	Anchor
■	310	403
✕	470	267
−	721	1047
○	905	258
▲	920	1048

Backstitch

	DMC	Anchor
◣	310	403

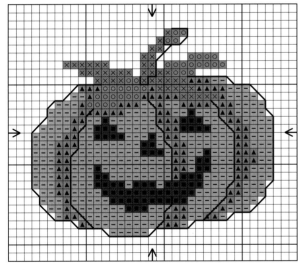

Measurements
The cross stitch design measures 6 x 7.5cm (2½ x 2⅞in)

Materials
- 15cm (6in) square of white 11-count Aida fabric
- One skein of stranded cotton in each colour listed in the key
- Size 24 tapestry needle
- Dark green single-fold card blank measuring 11.5 x 18cm
  (4½ x 7in)

Stitch details
Cross stitch use 3 strands
Backstitch use 2 strands

Note
When the stitching is complete, trim to eight Aida blocks
around the design. Fray two blocks and then stick on to
the card.

St Patrick's day

This wonderful Celtic knot cross, ideal as a card for someone who likes strong designs, is simple to stitch yet looks complex and sophisticated.

Measurements

The cross stitch design measures 8cm (3in) square

Materials

- 20cm (8in) square of holly green 14-count Aida fabric
- One skein of stranded cotton in each colour listed in the key
- Size 26 tapestry needle
- Dark green double-fold card blank measuring 15 x 20cm (6 x 8in) with a 10cm (4in) square aperture

Stitch details

Cross stitch use 2 strands
Backstitch use 1 strand

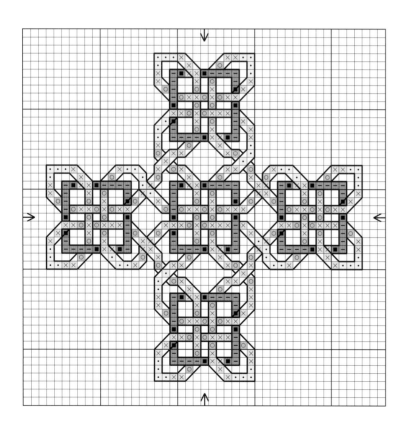

Key

	DMC	Anchor
−	321	46
○	783	307
■	816	47
✕	3820	305
•	3822	311

Backstitch

	DMC	Anchor
＼	816	47

St Valentine's day

Keep your loved one guessing with this Victorian-styled, hand-stitched Valentine's Day card.

Measurements
The cross stitch design measures 8cm (3in) square

Materials
- 13cm (5in) square of antique white 27-count evenweave fabric
- One skein of stranded cotton in each colour listed in the key
- Size 26 tapestry needle
- Pink double-fold card blank measuring 13.5 x 13.5cm (5¼ x 5¼in) with a 8.5cm (3¼in) square aperture

Stitch details
Work each stitch over 2 fabric threads
Cross stitch use 2 strands
Backstitch use 1 strand

Note
Before you send this card, why not add a couple of drops of scent to add a further air of mystery?

Key

	DMC	Anchor
○	523	859
+	677	885
✕	962	75
−	963	73

Backstitch

	DMC	Anchor
╲	3051	861
╲	3350	65

Motifs and borders

A border of bright holly leaves or Christmas trees
will brighten a Christmas card, and a row of
pumpkins will make a Halloween card memorable.
Remember to choose colours that will enhance the
theme of your card – cheerful red and green for
Christmas and the New Year, for example, or
romantic pink and silver for St Valentine's day.

Key

	DMC	Anchor			DMC	Anchor
·	blanc	1		O	798	131
4	209	96		●	815	47
✗	321	46		N	991	217
◰	413	236		I	992	1072
T	666	334		+	3756	1037
✗	680	907		↑	3820	305
▼	699	246		Z	3831	63
△	702	245				
→	704	255		**Backstitch**		
H	721	1048			DMC	Anchor
S	722	1047		◲	413	236
U	741	304		◲	680	907
–	743	302		◲	699	246
I	745	300		◲	702	245
▣	777	43		◲	704	255
∩	783	307		◲	796	134
■	796	134		◲	3820	305

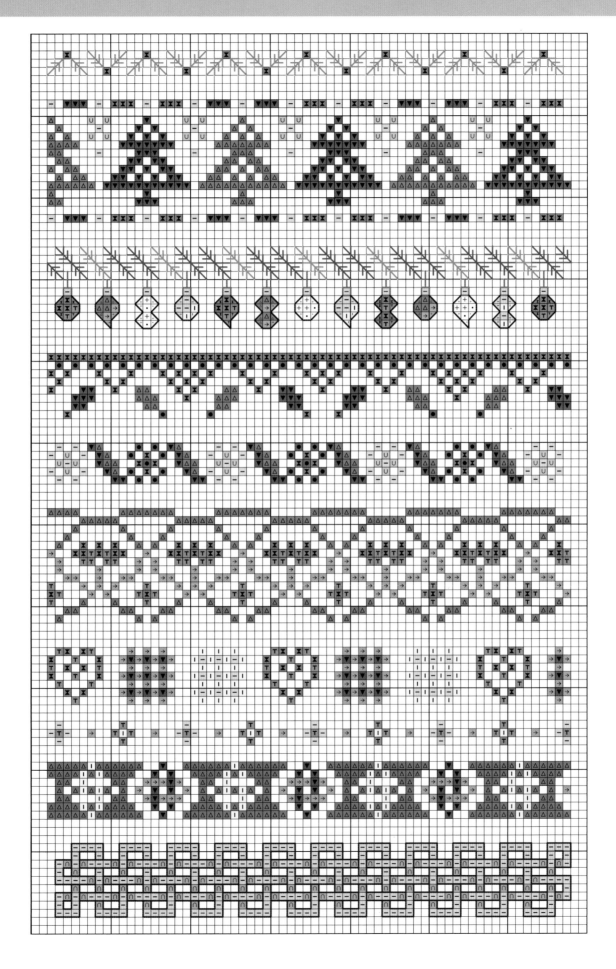

Flora and Fauna

Plants and animals are always popular subjects for cards. Flowers can be used in designs to suit every occasion. Animals can appear stylized, like the kittens and rabbits in this section, or more naturalistic, like the portrait of the horse.

Bluebells

Sunflowers

Lavender sachet

Rose water

Blueberry muffin

Apple pie

Art nouveau rose

Holly and ivy

Winter scene

Animal sampler

Horse

Puppy

Kitten

Rabbit

Motifs and borders

Bluebells

The bluebell is one of spring's most beautiful floral gems. When you see the rich blue flowers you know that summer is on its way.

Measurements

The cross stitch design measures 7.5 x 5cm (2⅞ x 2in)

Materials

- 13cm (5in) square of white 18-count Aida fabric
- One skein of stranded cotton in each colour listed in the key
- Size 26 tapestry needle
- Bright green double-fold card blank measuring 13 x 13cm (5 x 5in) with a 6 x 8cm (2½ x 3in) rectangular aperture

Stitch details

Cross stitch use 1 strand
Backstitch use 1 strand

Key					
	DMC	**Anchor**	**Backstitch**		
■	333	119		**DMC**	**Anchor**
○	793	118	◥	333	119
✕	989	265	◥	3346	267
−	3346	267			

Sunflowers

For a special floral greeting, stitch these bold sunflowers. Anyone receiving this card will be all sunny smiles.

Measurements

The cross stitch design measures 7 x 5cm (2¾ x 2in)

Materials

- 13cm (5in) square of white 18-count Aida fabric
- One skein of stranded cotton in each colour listed in the key
- Size 26 tapestry needle
- Yellow double-fold card blank measuring 13 x 10cm (5 x 4in) with a 5 x 8cm (2 x 3in) oval aperture

Note

If you use a lower-count fabric, you can turn this lovely design into a bigger picture, which could be framed or used to decorate the front of a fabric bag.

Key

	DMC	Anchor	Backstitch		
·	433	371	◣	433	371
✕	726	295	◣	3371	382
–	991	189			
○	993	186			
■	3371	382			

Stitch details

Cross stitch use 1 strand
Backstitch use 1 strand

Lavender sachet

Revive memories of the heavenly scent of lavender
with this charming picture of a traditional sachet
and sprig of flowers.

Measurements
The cross stitch design measures 10 x 7.5cm (4 x 2⅞in)

Materials
- 20cm (8in) square of white 28-count Zweigart Brittney evenweave fabric
- One skein of stranded cotton in each colour listed in the key
- Size 26 tapestry needle
- Lilac double-fold card blank measuring 14.5 x 20cm (5¾ x 8in) with a
  9.5 x 14.5cm (3¾ x 5¾in) oval aperture

Stitch details
Work each stitch over 2 fabric threads
Cross stitch use 2 strands
Backstitch use 1 strand

Key

	DMC	Anchor			DMC	Anchor
✕	340	108		−	3865	926
□	367	262		+	3866	2
○	958	186				
I	3033	387		**Backstitch**		
N	3364	859			DMC	Anchor
T	3746	98		＼	924	683
✳	3838	176		＼	3746	98

Rose water

This attractive rose and perfume bottle design is a delightful companion for the lavender sachet card opposite.

Measurements

The cross stitch design measures 10 x 7.5cm (4 x 2⅞in)

Materials

• 20cm (8in) square of white 28-count Zweigart Brittney evenweave fabric
• One skein of stranded cotton in each colour listed in the key
• Size 26 tapestry needle
• Pale pink double-fold card blank measuring 14.5 x 20cm (5¾ x 8in) with a 9.5 x 14.5cm (3¾ x 5¾in) oval aperture

Stitch details

Work each stitch over 2 fabric threads
Cross stitch use 2 strands
Backstitch use 1 strand

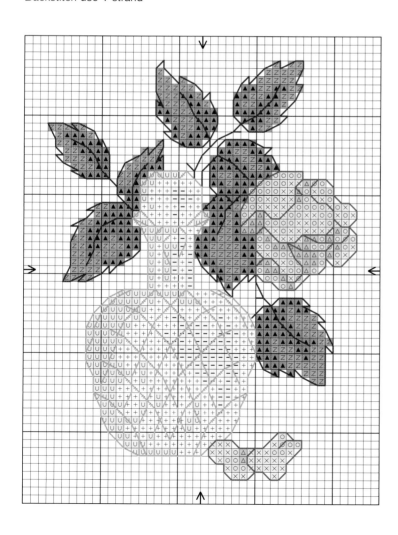

Key

	DMC	Anchor		DMC	Anchor
▲	367	262	+	3866	2
✕	761	23			
△	961	40	**Backstitch**		
U	3033	387		DMC	Anchor
Z	3364	859	╲	150	42
O	3708	25	╲	895	1044
−	3865	926	╲	961	40

Blueberry muffin

You can almost smell the aroma of baking with this
unusual design. The blueberries are a reminder of the
source of this delicious teatime treat.

Measurements

The cross stitch design measures 10.5 x 7.5cm (4¼ x 2⅞in)

Materials

- 20cm (8in) square of Rustico 14-count Aida fabric
- One skein of stranded cotton in each colour listed in the key
- Size 26 tapestry needle
- Violet single-fold card blank measuring 11.5 x 18cm (4⅝ x 7in)

Stitch details

Cross stitch use 2 strands
Backstitch use 1 strand

Note

When the stitching is complete, trim to six Aida blocks around
the design. Fray two blocks and then stick on to the card.

Key						
	DMC	**Anchor**			**DMC**	**Anchor**
+	blanc	1		■	987	861
T	333	99		U	989	265
O	435	369		−	3024	397
↑	436	362				
X	502	876		**Backstitch**		
▲	550	102			**DMC**	**Anchor**
□	792	941		◣	939	152
△	840	1084		◣	3021	1088
N	939	152				

Apple pie

This is a positively mouthwatering design to give to anyone who loves home baking.

Measurements

The cross stitch design measures 9.5 x 10.5cm (3¾ x 4¼in)

Materials

- 20cm (8in) square of Rustico 14-count Aida fabric
- One skein of stranded cotton in each colour listed in the key
- Size 26 tapestry needle
- Dark green single-fold card blank measuring 14.5cm (5¾in) square

Stitch details

Cross stitch use 2 strands
Backstitch use 1 strand

Note

When the stitching is complete, trim to six Aida blocks around the design. Fray two blocks and then stick on to the card.

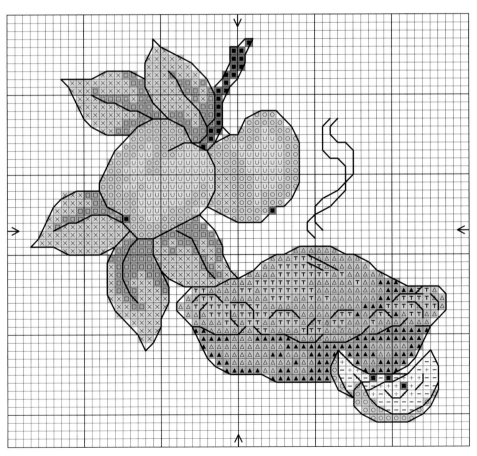

Key

	DMC	Anchor
+	blanc	1
□	320	859
×	368	260
▲	435	369
△	436	362
T	437	361
U	472	253
−	712	2
■	3021	1088
O	3348	264

Backstitch

	DMC	Anchor
╲	3021	1088

Art nouveau rose

This stylish, almost symmetrical rose motif makes an attractive card. The border of pulled threads adds another dimension to the finished design.

Measurements

The cross stitch design measures 10.5 x 8cm (4¼ x 3¼in)

Materials

- 20cm (8in) square of lilac 32-count Zweigart Belfast linen
- One skein of stranded cotton in each colour listed in the key
- Size 26 tapestry needle
- Violet single-fold card blank measuring 15 x 20cm (6 x 8in)

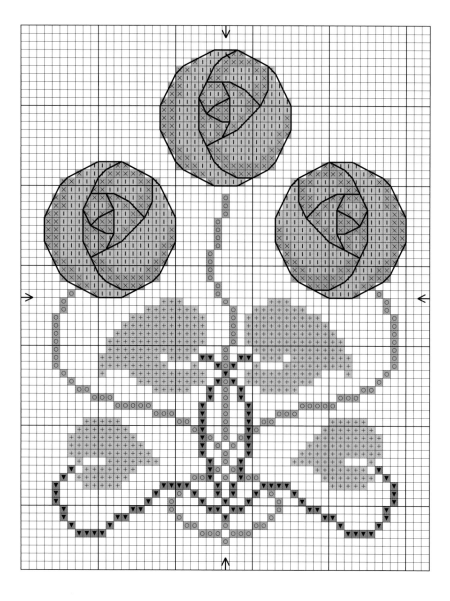

Stitch details

Work each stitch over 2 fabric threads
Cross stitch use 2 strands
Backstitch use 1 strand

Note

When the stitching is complete, trim the fabric to 2cm (¾in) around the design. Pull a single thread 1cm (½in) away from the motif, leave four threads in place, then pull another thread. Repeat on the other three sides. Finally, fray the edges and stick on to the card.

Key

	DMC	Anchor
+	959	185
×	3687	76
I	3688	74
○	3815	209
▼	3847	1076

Backstitch

	DMC	Anchor
╲	3834	972

Holly and ivy

Christmas wouldn't be Christmas without some holly and ivy. Add this festive card to the decorations on your mantelpiece.

Measurements

The cross stitch design measures 6.5 x 5.5cm (2⅝ x 2¼in)

Materials

- 13cm (5in) square of white 18-count Aida fabric
- One skein of stranded cotton in each colour listed in the key
- Size 26 tapestry needle
- Green double-fold card blank measuring 13 x 13cm (5 x 5in) with a 7 x 8cm (2¾ x 3in) rectangular aperture

Stitch details

Cross stitch use 1 strand
Backstitch use 1 strand

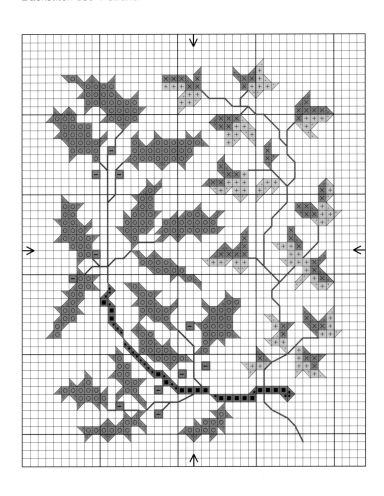

Note

You can use red seed beads for the berries on this card to add an unusual and effective touch.

Key

	DMC	Anchor	Backstitch		
				DMC	Anchor
✕	469	267			
+	472	278	╲	469	267
–	817	19	╲	817	19
■	319	217	╲	319	217
○	699	229			

Winter scene

A snow-covered landscape always looks beautiful. Snow-peaked roofs conjure up an idyllic image of crisp winter days.

Measurements

The cross stitch design measures 7 x 5.5cm (2¾ x 2¼in)

Materials

- 13cm (5in) square of white 18-count Aida fabric
- One skein of stranded cotton in each colour listed in the key
- Kreinik blending filament
- Size 26 tapestry needle
- Lavender double-fold card blank measuring 13 x 13cm (5 x 5in) with a 7 x 8cm (2¾ x 3in) rectangular aperture

Stitch details

Cross stitch use 1 strand

Backstitch use 1 strand

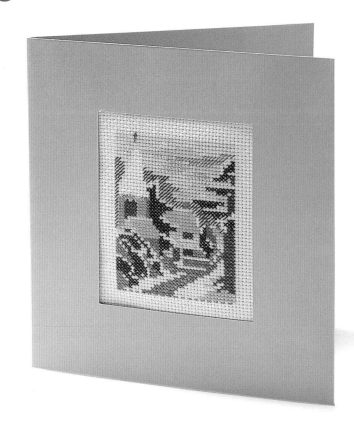

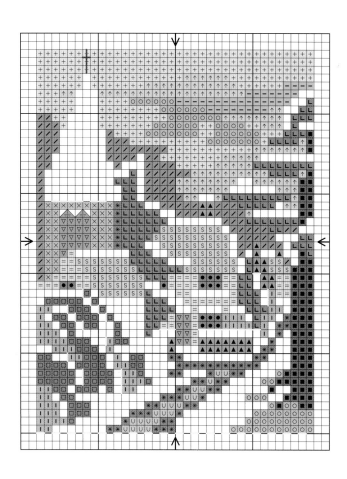

Key

	DMC	Anchor
▽	208	111
U	210	109
■	300	357
⬚	501	878
I	503	876
✕	613	853
L	699	923
S	742	303
○	794	120
●	797	132
✳	3011	856
▲	3350	77
=	3689	73

Half cross stitch

	DMC	Anchor
+	794	120
╱	797	132
−	3350	77
↑	3354	74

Backstitch

	DMC	Anchor
╲	300	357

Kreinik metallic

☐	sky blue (014)

Animal sampler

If counting sheep appeals to you, why not try counting pigs, chickens and ducks, too? This card would look fabulous framed and hung in a nursery.

Measurements

The cross stitch design measures 13.5 x 8.5cm (5¼ x 3¼in)

Materials

- 20 x 14.5cm (8 x 5¾in) of white 14-count Aida fabric
- One skein of stranded cotton in each colour listed in the key
- Size 26 tapestry needle
- Pink double-fold card blank measuring 12.5 x 20cm (5 x 8in) with a 9.5 x 14.5cm (3¾ x 5¾in) rectangular aperture

Stitch details

Cross stitch use 2 strands
Backstitch use 1 strand

Note

Individual animal motifs taken from this chart could be used to make gift tags or small items such as fridge magnets or keyrings.

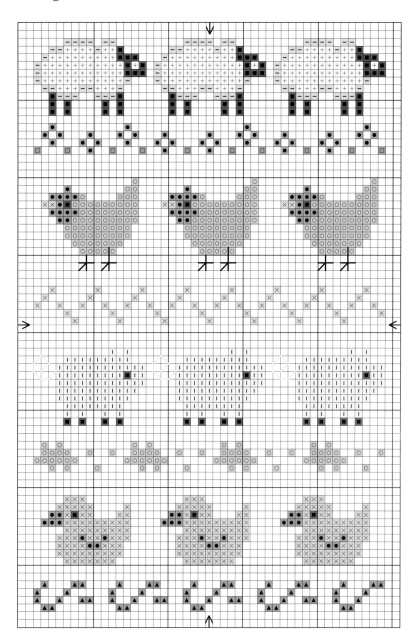

Key

	DMC	Anchor			DMC	Anchor
■	310	403		I	3689	49
−	318	399		+	blanc	1
▲	322	978				
●	347	13		**Backstitch**		
○	436	363			DMC	Anchor
×	725	306		╲	310	403
▣	911	230		╲	3689	49

Horse

This simple yet striking study of a horse's head makes an ideal card for any equestrian enthusiast, young or old.

Measurements
The cross stitch design measures 7.5 x 9.5cm (2⅞ x 3¾in)

Materials
- 20cm (8in) square of Rustico 14-count Aida fabric
- One skein of stranded cotton in each colour listed in the key
- Size 26 tapestry needle
- Cream double-fold card blank measuring 15 x 20cm (6 x 8in) with a 9.5 x 14.5cm (3¾ x 5⅝in) oval aperture

Stitch details
Cross stitch use 2 strands
Backstitch use 1 strand

Key

	DMC	Anchor		DMC	Anchor
·	blanc	1	■	3371	382
○	433	358			
✕	434	370	**Backstitch**		
I	435	369		DMC	Anchor
+	712	2	◤	3371	382
▲	938	380			

Puppy

This cute little puppy has plenty to chew on! If you know someone who has recently acquired a new companion, this card will make a perfect gift.

Key

	DMC	Anchor			DMC	Anchor
+	blanc	1		I	3840	128
⊙	434	370				
–	712	2		**Backstitch**		
✕	726	295			DMC	Anchor
▣	930	1036		◣	938	380
■	938	380				

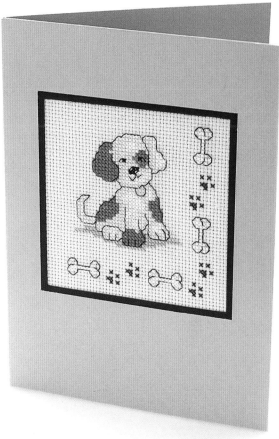

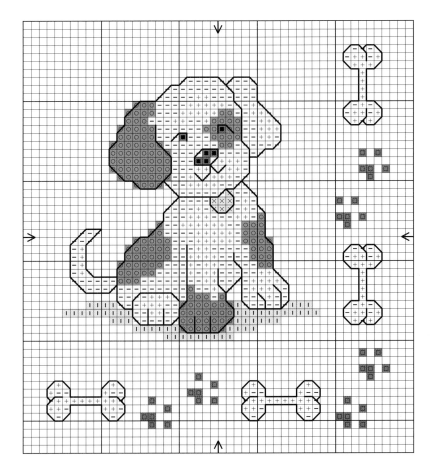

Measurements
The cross stitch design measures 9cm (3½in) square

Materials
- 20cm (8in) square of ice blue 14-count Aida fabric
- One skein of stranded cotton in each colour listed in the key
- Size 26 tapestry needle
- Blue double-fold card blank measuring 15 x 20cm (6 x 8in) with an 11cm (4¼in) square aperture
- 13cm (5in) square of brown card

Stitch details
Cross stitch use 2 strands
Backstitch use 1 strand

Note
Cut an aperture in the square of brown card so that it is slightly smaller than the one in the card blank. Stick it to the inside of the card to create a stylish double-mount effect. Then mount the finished stitching in the usual way.

Kitten

What more could a cat lover want than this playful little kitten framed by a border of toy mice?

Measurements
The cross stitch design measures 7cm (2¾in) square

Materials
- 15cm (6in) square of cream 14-count Aida fabric
- One skein of stranded cotton in each colour listed in the key
- Size 26 tapestry needle
- Baby pink double-fold card blank measuring 10.5 x 15cm (4⅛ x 6in) with an 8.5cm (3¼in) square aperture
- 10cm (4in) square of brown card

Stitch details
Cross stitch use 2 strands
Backstitch use 1 strand

Note
Cut an aperture in the square of brown card so that it is slightly smaller than the one in the card blank. Stick it to the inside of the card to create a stylish double-mount effect. Then mount the finished stitching in the usual way.

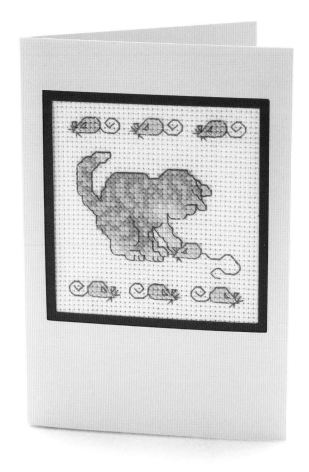

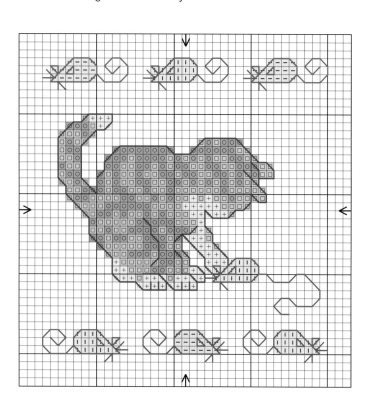

Key

	DMC	Anchor	Backstitch		
				DMC	Anchor
□	437	368			
+	739	366	◥	300	358
I	3609	103	◥	718	88
○	3776	1048	◥	798	131
–	3840	128			

Rabbit

This cheeky little bunny has turned his back on us – no doubt to concentrate on the border of delicious carrots that surround him!

Measurements

The cross stitch design measures 8 x 6cm (3 x 2½in)

Materials

- 15cm (6in) square of mint green 32-count linen
- One skein of stranded cotton in each colour listed in the key
- Size 26 tapestry needle
- White single-fold card blank measuring 11.5 x 18cm (4⅜ x 7in)

Stitch details

Work each stitch over 2 fabric threads

Cross stitch use 2 strands

Backstitch use 1 strand

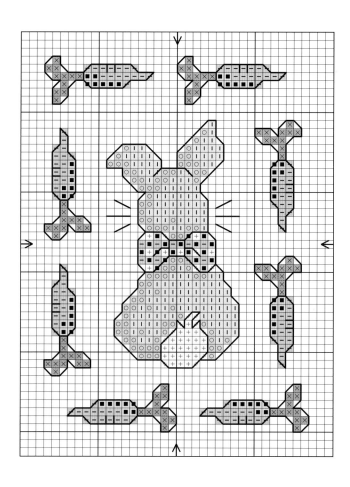

Note

When stitching is complete, pull a single thread 0.5cm (¼in) away from the motif, leaving 4 threads in place. Trim the fabric, fray the edges and then stick on to the card.

Key

	DMC	Anchor
+	blanc	1
○	318	398
I	415	397
–	741	314
■	743	311
✕	988	266

Backstitch

	DMC	Anchor
◥	413	236

Motifs and borders

Floral borders, with swags of twining stems and branches, are always decorative additions to a design, and patterns of alternating motifs, such as the flowers and fruits shown here, are equally attractive. Larger motifs, such as these charming pigs or bold cockerels, can be used on their own or combined to make more traditional sampler-style designs.

Key

	DMC	Anchor			DMC	Anchor
·	blanc	1		S	3326	73
●	221	896		▼	3685	69
▣	333	112		4	3747	128
○	340	108		✕	3834	972
★	349	334				
I	351	328		**Backstitch**		
∪	472	253			DMC	Anchor
∩	676	361		＼	221	896
─	680	907		＼	333	112
I	743	302		＼	340	108
↑	745	300		＼	680	907
→	818	271		＼	987	861
Z	987	861		＼	3021	1088
H	989	265		＼	3685	69
T	3021	1088		＼	3834	972

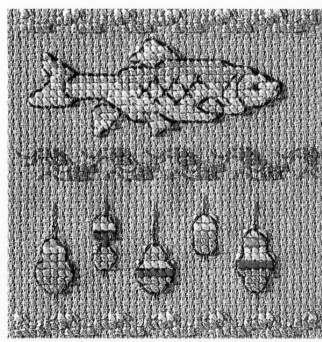

Hobbies and Special Interests

A card that contains a reference to a favourite pastime or hobby is sure to be welcome. If friends or relatives enjoy gardening or fishing or have a special interest in woodworking, stitch the appropriate design for them.

Garden tools sampler

Tools sampler

Sewing sampler

Fishing sampler

Transport sampler

Lighthouse sampler

Delft tiles

Edwardian lady

Motifs and borders

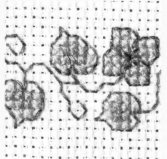

Garden tools sampler

A simple arrangement of garden tools and pretty
floral borders create an attractive garden sampler.

Measurements

The cross stitch design measures 10 x 7cm (4 x 2¾in)

Materials

• 20cm (8in) square of cream 16-count Aida fabric
• One skein of stranded cotton in each colour listed in the key
• Size 26 tapestry needle
• Purple double-fold card blank measuring 11.5 x 18cm (4⅝ x 7in)
  with a 7.5 x 11cm (2⅞ x 4¼in) rectangular aperture

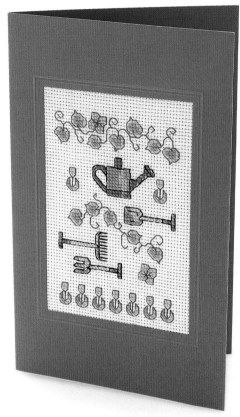

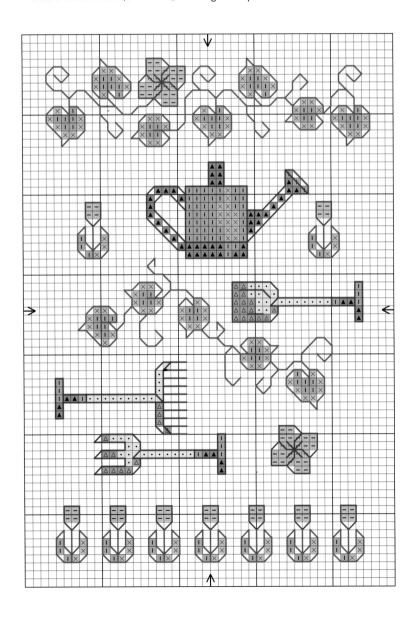

Stitch details

Cross stitch use 2 strands
Backstitch use 1 strand

Key

	DMC	Anchor
△	169	399
−	210	342
•	415	234
▲	987	262
I	989	265
×	3348	254

Backstitch

	DMC	Anchor
╲	327	100
╲	939	152
╲	987	262

Tools sampler

Woodworking enthusiasts like nothing better than a good collection of top-quality tools – and here it is!

Measurements

The cross stitch design measures 10 x 7cm (4 x 2¾in)

Materials

- 20cm (8in) square of white 16-count Aida fabric
- One skein of stranded cotton in each colour listed in the key
- Size 26 tapestry needle
- Dark red double-fold card blank measuring 11.5 x 18cm (4⅜ x 7in) with a 7.5 x 11cm (2⅞ x 4¼in) rectangular aperture

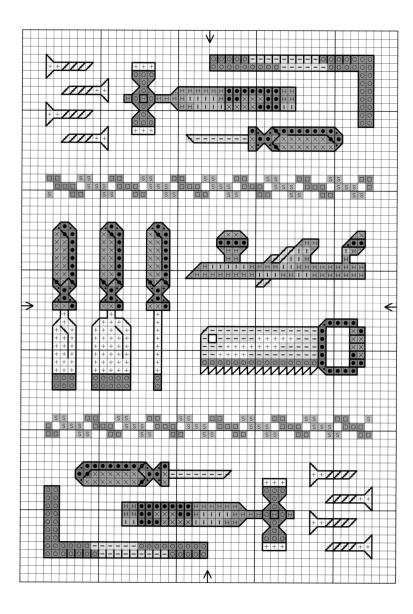

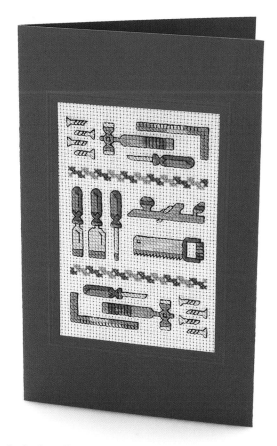

Stitch details

Cross stitch use 2 strands
Backstitch use 1 strand

Key

	DMC	Anchor		DMC	Anchor
●	355	339	+	762	2
×	356	337	□	3809	1066
○	414	398			
−	415	234	**Backstitch**		
H	435	370		DMC	Anchor
I	436	369	╲	3799	400
S	597	1062			

Sewing sampler

This is a stunning little study of the 'tools of the trade', which you might want to stitch for yourself to remind you of the pleasures of sewing.

Measurements

The cross stitch design measures 10 x 7cm (4 x 2¾in)

Materials

- 20cm (8in) square of cream 16-count Aida fabric
- One skein of stranded cotton in each colour listed in the key
- Size 26 tapestry needle
- Antique pink double-fold card blank measuring 11.5 x 18cm (4⅜ x 7in) with a 7.5 x 11cm (2⅞ x 4¼in) rectangular aperture

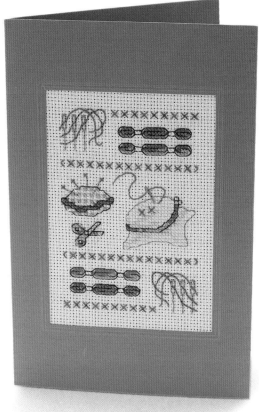

Stitch details

Cross stitch use 2 strands
Backstitch refer to key

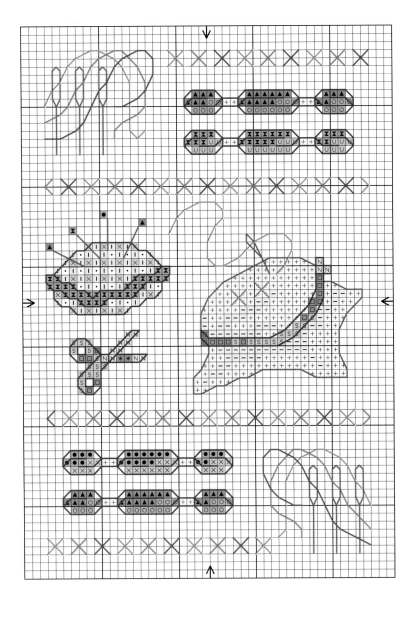

Key

	DMC	Anchor
·	blanc	1
X	208	98
U	209	96
*	414	235
N	415	234
□	434	370
S	436	362
O	518	168
●	602	63
X	603	55
I	605	103
−	828	158
+	3756	1037

	DMC	Anchor
▲	3760	169

Backstitch using 1 strand

	DMC	Anchor
◢	3021	1088

Backstitch using 2 strands

	DMC	Anchor
◢	208	98
◢	414	235
◢	602	63
◢	3760	169

Fishing sampler

This unusual sampler is the ideal gift for a fisherman (or woman) of any age who likes to reminisce about 'the one that got away'.

Measurements

The cross stitch design measures 9 x 6.5cm (3½ x 2½in)

Materials

- 20cm (8in) square of sage 18-count Aida fabric
- One skein of stranded cotton in each colour listed in the key
- Size 26 tapestry needle
- Blue double-fold card blank measuring 11.5 x 18cm (4⅜ x 7in) with a 7.5 x 11cm (2⅞ x 4¼in) rectangular aperture

Stitch details

Cross stitch use 2 strands
Backstitch use 1 strand

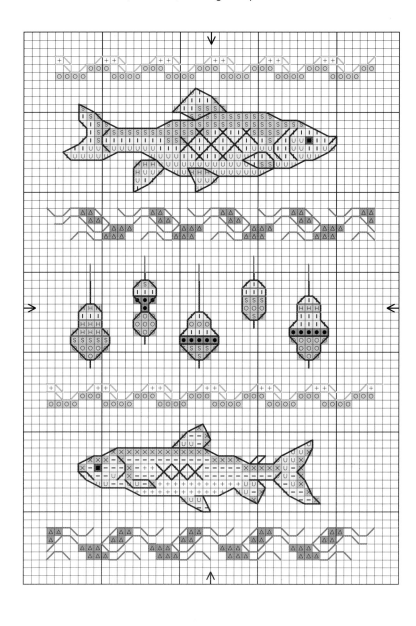

Key

	DMC	Anchor			DMC	Anchor
S	164	240		+	3866	2
O	519	167				
X	648	234		**Backstitch**		
●	666	334			DMC	Anchor
U	739	892		◥	519	167
△	988	266		◥	666	334
−	3072	926		◥	935	1044
I	3078	292		◥	988	266
H	3854	302				

Transport sampler

Take a nostalgic look at travel with this eclectic collection of old-fashioned methods of transportation.

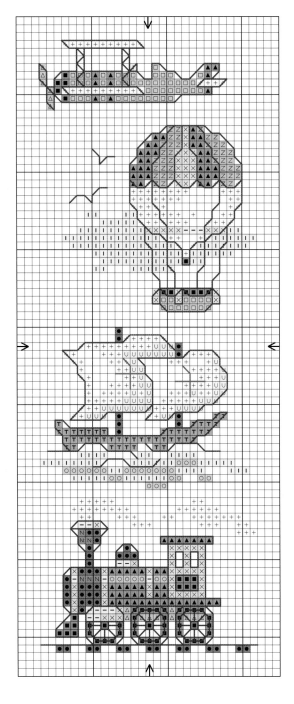

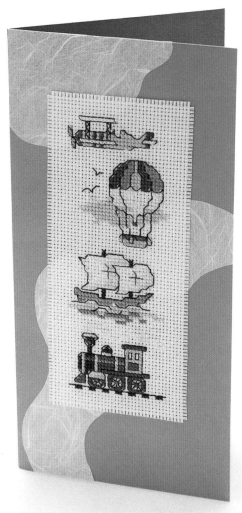

Key

	DMC	Anchor
Z	351	328
■	355	1014
T	435	369
□	437	368
N	646	399
△	648	234
+	712	2
U	739	366
O	813	159
▲	826	161
I	828	1037
●	844	1041
X	3820	311
−	3822	292

Backstitch

	DMC	Anchor
◻	355	1014
◻	844	1041

Measurements

The cross stitch design measures 13 x 5cm (5 x 2in)

Materials

- 20cm (8in) square of white 16-count Aida fabric
- One skein of stranded cotton in each colour listed in the key
- Size 26 tapestry needle
- Blue single-fold card blank measuring 10 x 20cm (4 x 8in)
- Semi-transparent paper

Stitch details

Cross stitch use 2 strands
Backstitch use 1 strand

Note

Cut swirls of semi-translucent paper to imitate clouds and stick them to the card blank first. When the stitching is complete, trim to six Aida blocks around the design. Fray one block and then stick on to the card.

Lighthouse sampler

This quaint lighthouse with its shell and starfish border makes
the perfect card for any seafarer.

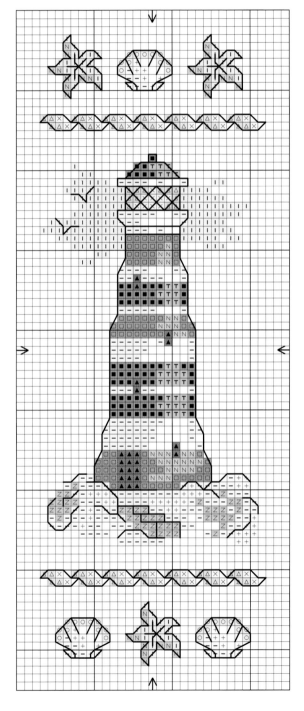

Key

	DMC	Anchor
■	349	334
T	351	328
Z	648	234
△	676	361
✕	677	386
+	712	2
○	761	271
N	813	159
□	826	161
I	828	1037
▲	844	1041
-	3072	926

Backstitch

	DMC	Anchor
＼	844	1041

Measurements
The cross stitch design measures 13 x 5cm (5 x 2in)

Materials
- 20cm (8in) square of white 16-count Aida fabric
- One skein of stranded cotton in each colour listed in the key
- Size 26 tapestry needle
- Blue single-fold card blank measuring 10 x 20cm (4 x 8in)
- Sandpaper

Stitch details
Cross stitch use 2 strands
Backstitch use 1 strand

Note
Cut some shapes from sandpaper and stick them to the
card blank. When the stitching is complete, trim to six Aida
blocks around the design. Fray one block and then stick on to
the card.

Delft tiles

These pretty little Dutch scenes are inspired by those depicted on Delft tiles, first produced in the Netherlands in the 17th century. Send this card to a friend or relative who collects blue-and-white ceramics.

Measurements

The cross stitch design measures 5.5 x 14.5cm (2¼ x 5¾in)

Materials

- 25cm (10in) square of white 16-count Aida fabric
- One skein of stranded cotton in each colour listed in the key
- Size 26 tapestry needle
- Blue single-fold card blank measuring 13 x 23cm (5 x 9in)

Stitch details

Cross stitch use 2 strands
Backstitch use 1 strand

Note

When the stitching is complete, trim to eight Aida blocks around the design. Fray two blocks and then stick on to the card.

Key		
	DMC	Anchor
■	796	134
⊙	798	131
✕	799	130
−	800	1037

Backstitch		
	DMC	Anchor
◥	796	134

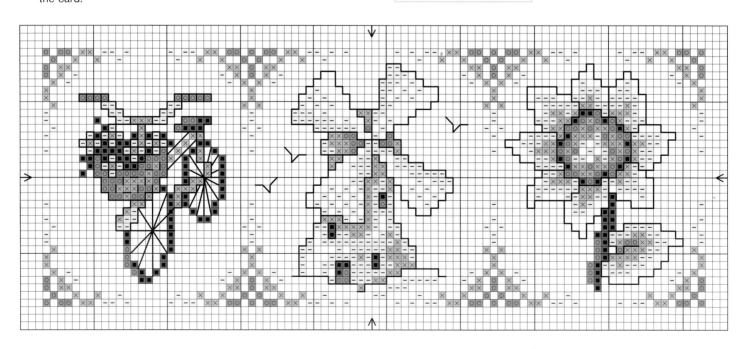

Edwardian lady

If you are an experienced stitcher, this portrait of a stylish Edwardian lady shows how depth and texture can be created using delicate shading.

Measurements

The cross stitch design measures 13.5 x 7.5cm (5¼ x 2⅞in)

Materials

- 25cm (10in) square of cream 28-count Zweigart Brittney evenweave fabric
- One skein of stranded cotton in each colour listed in the key
- Size 26 tapestry needle
- Cream double-fold card blank measuring 15 x 20cm (6 x 8in) with an 11 x 15.5cm (4¼ x 6¼in) rectangular aperture
- 14 x 19cm (5½ x 7½in) of rich purple card

Stitch details

Work each stitch over 2 fabric threads
Cross stitch use 2 strands
Backstitch use 1 strand

Note

Cut an aperture in the purple card so that it is slightly smaller than the one in the card blank. Stick it to the inside of the card to create a stylish double-mount effect. Then mount the finished stitching in the usual way.

Key

	DMC	Anchor
+	blanc	1
Z	208	98
I	209	96
□	367	262
▲	400	310
×	597	167
■	924	683
U	928	847
H	989	265
O	3712	9
-	3756	1037
·	3770	271
I	3774	1011
L	3776	1048
●	3808	1066
▽	3810	1064
→	3822	292

Backstitch

	DMC	Anchor
\	924	683
\	3772	1007
\	3822	292

Motifs and borders

Combine the motifs here to create a card for a motoring enthusiast or someone whose passion is woodworking. Unusual borders, created from a pattern of screws or garden forks, will make your cards individual and completely unforgettable.

Key

	DMC	Anchor			DMC	Anchor
·	blanc	1		+	762	2
✕	209	96		✗	987	861
4	210	103		−	989	265
●	355	1014		⊡	3760	169
Z	356	1013		■	3799	400
☐	414	235				
S	415	234		**Backstitch**		
T	434	370			DMC	Anchor
○	436	362		╲	209	96
△	518	168		╲	210	103
I	519	167		╲	414	235
▼	602	63		╲	519	167
N	603	55		╲	602	63
↑	605	103		╲	989	265
∩	726	295		╲	3760	169
→	727	292		╲	3799	400

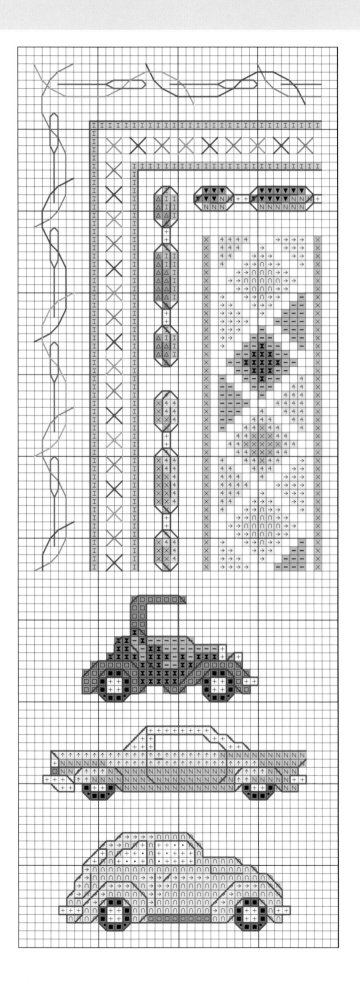

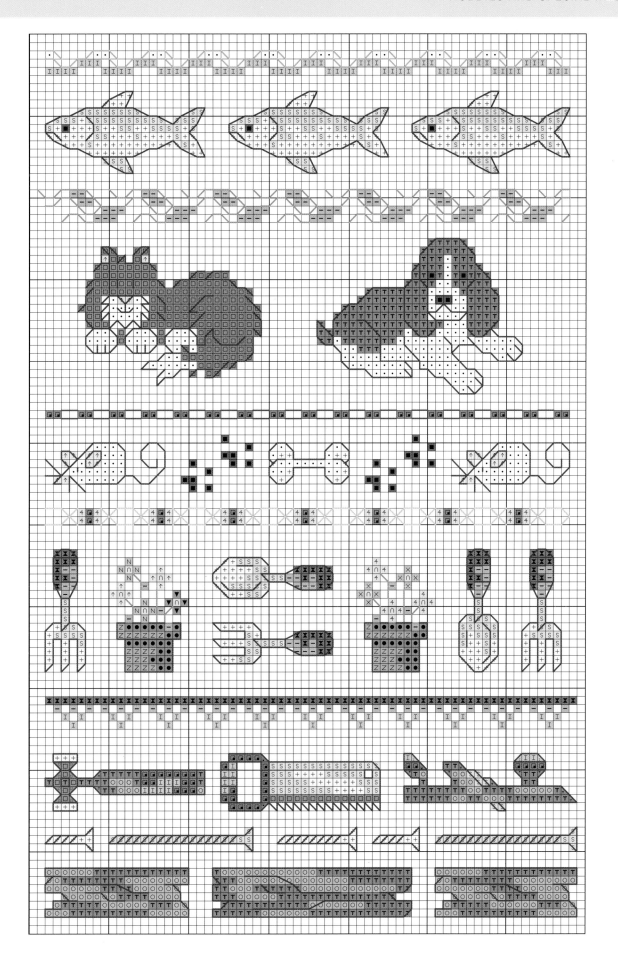

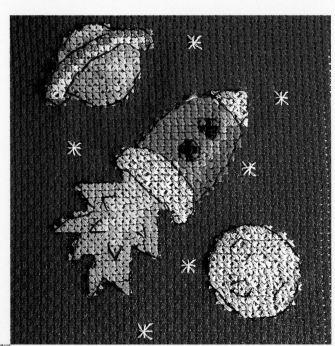

Children's Themes

Animals are always popular with children, and the designs in this section include some delightful bears, a cheerful giraffe and a traditional rocking horse. There is also an underwater theme, as well as a spacescape for a budding astronaut.

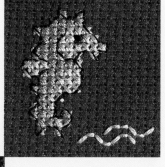

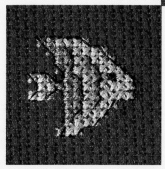

Elephants

This young elephant is hanging on tightly to his mother's tail, making this an ideal card to reinforce the message that an independent-minded toddler should hold tight to mummy's hand.

Key

	DMC	Anchor
+	blanc	1
×	210	96
I	211	103
−	747	158
U	800	128
O	809	120
✳	3839	144

Backstitch

	DMC	Anchor
╲	797	133
╲	3837	99

Measurements

The cross stitch design measures 5.5 x 12.5cm (2¼ x 4¾in)

Materials

• 20cm (8in) square of white 14-count Aida fabric
• One skein of stranded cotton in each colour listed in the key
• Size 26 tapestry needle
• Pink single-fold card blank measuring 10 x 21cm (4 x 8½in)

Stitch details

Cross stitch use 2 strands
Backstitch use 1 strand

Note

When the stitching is complete, trim to six Aida blocks around the design. Fray two blocks and then stick on to the card.

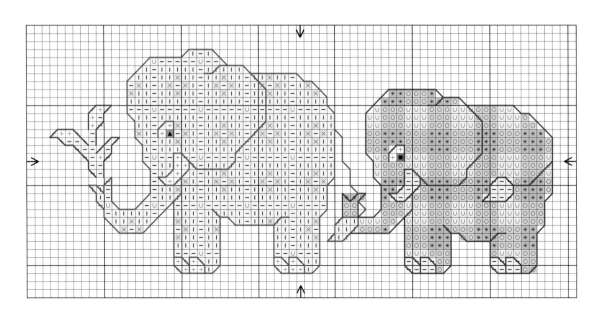

Giraffe

Giraffes are gentle creatures, and this one seems
to have a sense of humour, too! She would make a
lovely gift for any young child.

Key

	DMC	Anchor		French knots	
+	blanc	1		**DMC**	**Anchor**
o	301	1049	×	383	798
·	744	301			
■	3777	340			

Backstitch

	DMC	Anchor
╲	3777	340

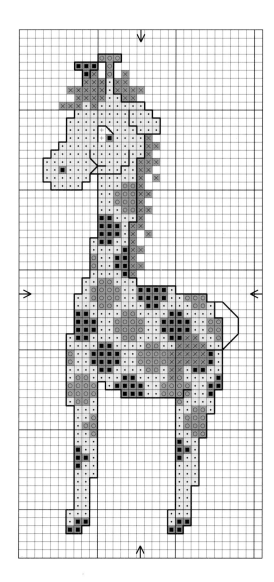

Measurements

The cross stitch design measures 11.5 x 5cm
(4⅝ x 2in)

Materials

- 20cm (8in) square of peach 28-count Zweigart
  Cashel linen
- One skein of stranded cotton in each colour listed in
  the key
- Size 26 tapestry needle
- Violet double-fold card blank measuring 20 x 15cm
  (8 x 5¾in) with a 9.5 x 14.5cm (3¾ x 5¾in) oval
  aperture

Stitch details

Work each stitch over 2 fabric threads
Cross stitch use 2 strands
Backstitch use 1 strand
French knots use 3 strands

Children's toys

Why not make a card that's as much a gift as it is a greeting? You could frame this nursery design, and it would provide a welcome and long-lasting reminder of childhood.

Measurements

The cross stitch design measures 8.5 x 12cm (3¼ x 4½in)

Materials

- 14.5 x 20cm (5¾ x 8in) of white 14-count Aida fabric
- One skein of stranded cotton in each colour listed in the key
- Size 26 tapestry needle
- Yellow double-fold card blank measuring 15 x 20cm (6 x 8in) with a 10 x 15cm (4 x 6in) rectangular aperture

Stitch details

Cross stitch use 2 strands
Backstitch refer to key
French knots use 1 strand

Note

You can use the alphabets and numbers on pages 110–11 to personalize this card with a name and date of birth.

Key

	DMC	Anchor
•	Blanc	1
O	224	894
→	225	892
■	310	403
X	321	9046
▽	334	977
×	402	347
L	413	401
+	445	288
−	471	265
↑	677	300
T	701	245
U	726	297
▲	797	132
S	3072	397
I	3326	24
△	3607	87

Backstitch using 1 strand

	DMC	Anchor
＼	317	400
＼	433	357

Backstitch using 2 strands

	DMC	Anchor
＼	310	403
＼	321	9046

French knots

	DMC	Anchor
✳	317	400

Toy sampler

Remember how pleased you would have been to receive a card like this when you were young? Or, better still, the toys themselves!

Measurements
The cross stitch design measures 8.5 x 12.5cm (3¼ x 4¾in)

Materials
- 14.5 x 20cm (5¾ x 8in) of white 14-count Aida fabric
- One skein of stranded cotton in each colour listed in the key
- Size 26 tapestry needle
- Red double-fold card blank measuring 15 x 20cm (6 x 8cm) with a 10.5 x 14.5cm (4⅛ x 5¾in) rectangular aperture

Stitch details
Cross stitch use 2 strands
Backstitch use 1 strand

Note
If you have untold patience and want a really challenging project, why not repeat this design to make a stunning fabric shelf border for a child's room? For a larger project still, you could use it as the mainstay of a room design.

Key

	DMC	Anchor
■	310	403
▲	322	978
●	347	13
▢	435	901
−	436	363
Ι	562	210
✕	563	208
·	677	300
+	726	295
○	809	130
△	3689	49

Backstitch

	DMC	Anchor
╲	310	403
╲	322	978
╲	347	403
╲	435	9046

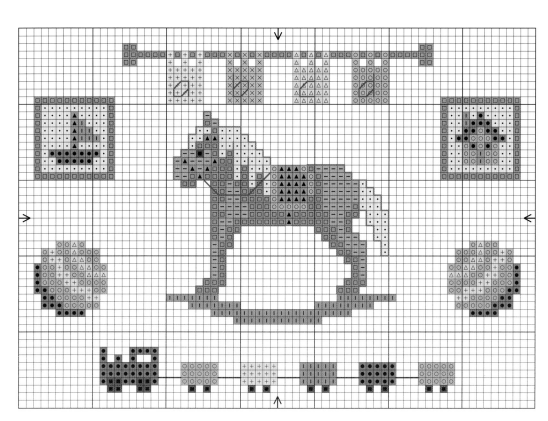

Cuddly bears

These adorable little bears are the perfect example of friendship, and they will make a lovely card to give to siblings.

Measurements
The cross stitch design measures 6 x 5.5cm (2½ x 2¼in)

Materials
- 15cm (6in) square of cream 18-count Aida fabric
- One skein of stranded cotton in each colour listed in the key
- Size 26 tapestry needle
- Powder blue single-fold card blank measuring 11.5 x 18cm (4⅜ x 7in)

Stitch details
Cross stitch use 1 strand
Backstitch use 1 strand

Note
You could stitch one of the borders from pages 102–3 to add extra charm to the design. When the stitching is complete, trim to eight Aida blocks around the design. Fray two blocks and then stick on to the card.

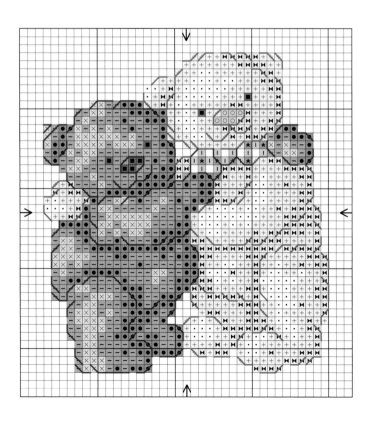

Key

	DMC	Anchor		DMC	Anchor
·	blanc	1	■	838	380
+	ecru	276	–	3828	1045
●	420	1046			
○	644	391	**Backstitch**		
×	738	363		DMC	Anchor
⋈	739	1080	╲	420	375
I	813	120	╲	838	380
★	826	161			

Bear repeat

This cute teddy bear design is perfect for twins, but it can be adapted for one child or even for triplets.

Measurements
The cross stitch design measures 6 x 11.5cm (2½ x 4⅜in)

Materials
- 13 x 15cm (5 x 6in) of white 18-count Aida fabric
- One skein of stranded cotton in each colour listed in the key
- Size 26 tapestry needle
- Pale green double-fold card blank measuring 10 x 15cm (4 x 6in) with a 7 x 11.5cm (2¾ x 4⅜in) rectangular aperture

Stitch details
Cross stitch use 1 strand
Backstitch use 1 strand

Note
Choose the appropriate number and combination of girl or boy bears to suit the twins or triplets for whom you are stitching.

Key

	DMC	Anchor	Backstitch		
				DMC	Anchor
−	563	208	◥	310	403
!	676	891	◥	781	309
□	729	890			
●	781	309			
○	809	130			
✕	3354	74			
+	3822	305			

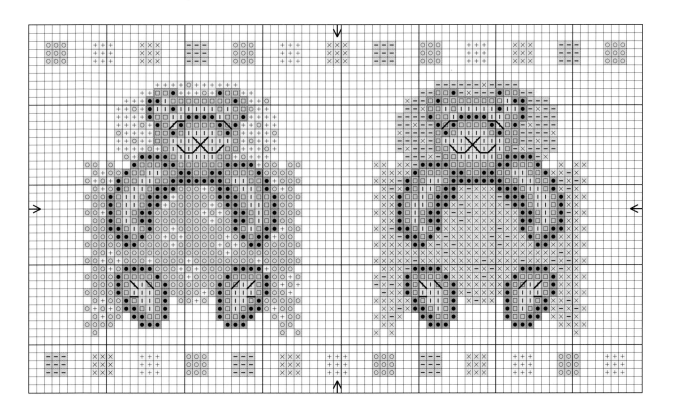

Clown

This jolly clown is ready to bring lots of fun to a child's birthday party or to another special event.

Measurements

The cross stitch design measures 9 x 5.5cm (3½ x 2¼in)

Materials

- 20cm (8in) square of orange 14-count Aida fabric
- One skein of stranded cotton in each colour listed in the key
- Size 26 tapestry needle
- Bright blue double-fold card blank measuring 15 x 20cm (6 x 8in) with a 10cm (4in) square aperture

Stitch details

Cross stitch use 2 strands
Backstitch use 1 strand
Straight stitch use 2 strands

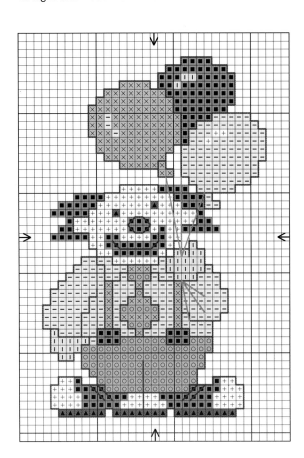

Key

	DMC	Anchor
+	blanc	1
▲	154	72
■	326	39
×	704	255
−	727	289
I	761	49
O	3843	433

Backstitch

	DMC	Anchor
＼	154	72

Straight stitch

	DMC	Anchor
＼	3843	433

Ballerina

At some time or other most little girls dream of becoming a ballerina. Make a dream come true with this delightful pretty-in-pink picture.

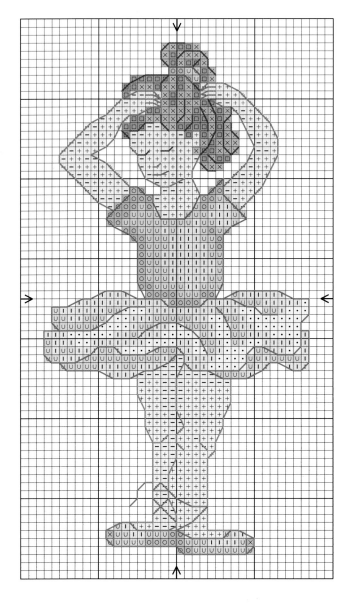

Measurements

The cross stitch design measures 12 x 7 (4½ x 2¾in)

Materials

- 25cm (10in) square of white 14-count Aida fabric
- One skein of stranded cotton in each colour listed in the key
- Size 26 tapestry needle
- White double-fold card blank measuring 15 x 20cm (6 x 8in) with a 9.5 x 14.5cm (3¾ x 5¾in) oval aperture

Stitch details

Cross stitch use 2 strands
Backstitch use 1 strand

Key

	DMC	Anchor	Backstitch		
				DMC	Anchor
▣	435	369			
✕	436	362	◥	309	63
○	603	55	◥	801	358
∪	604	23	◥	3859	895
I	605	103			
·	818	271			
+	3770	1009			
−	3774	881			

Racing car

Impress the car enthusiast in the family with
this striking sports car.

Measurements

The cross stitch design measures
10 x 5.5cm (4 x 2¼in)

Materials

• 20cm (8in) square of white 14-count
  Aida fabric
• One skein of stranded cotton in each
  colour listed in the key
• Size 26 tapestry needle
• Green double-fold card blank measuring
  11.5 x 18cm (4⅜ x 7in) with a 7.5 x 11cm
  (2⅞ x 4¼in) rectangular aperture

Stitch details

Cross stitch use 2 strands
Backstitch use 1 strand

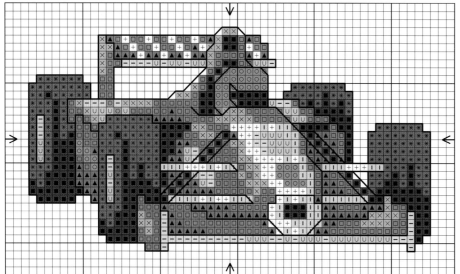

Key

	DMC	Anchor
+	blanc	1
■	310	403
⊡	349	334
×	351	328
✳	413	236
I	415	234
▲	498	13
○	703	256
–	726	295
U	742	298

Backstitch

	DMC	Anchor
╲	310	403

Football star

This bold collection of soccer motifs is sure to please any budding football star.

Measurements

The cross stitch design measures 6 x 10cm (2½ x 4in)

Materials

- 15cm (6in) square of bright green 14-count Aida fabric
- One skein of stranded cotton in each colour listed in the key
- Size 26 tapestry needle
- Red double-fold card blank measuring 10.5 x 15cm (4⅛ x 6in) with a 7 x 11cm (2¾ x 4¼in) rectangular aperture

Stitch details

Cross stitch use 2 strands
Backstitch use 1 strand

Note

If you want to attribute the shirt to a favourite team, simply alter the colours to match their strip.

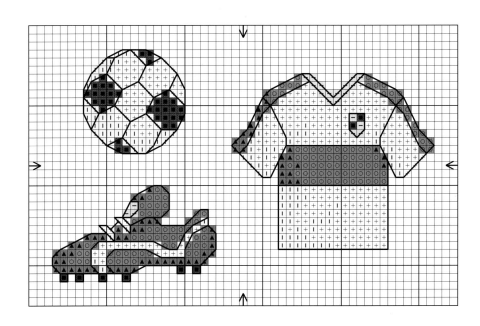

Key

	DMC	Anchor
+	blanc	1
■	310	403
○	349	334
▲	498	13
−	727	292
I	762	2

Backstitch

	DMC	Anchor
╲	310	403

Ocean scene

Explore the wonders of the ocean with this fun collection of underwater motifs.

Measurements

The cross stitch design measures 9 x 7cm (3½ x 2¾in)

Materials

- 20cm (8in) square of navy 14-count Aida fabric
- One skein of stranded cotton in each colour listed in the key
- Size 26 tapestry needle
- Yellow double-fold card blank measuring 11.5 x 18cm (4⅜ x 7in) with a 7.5 x 11cm (2⅞ x 4¼in) rectangular aperture

Stitch details

Cross stitch use 2 strands
Backstitch refer to key

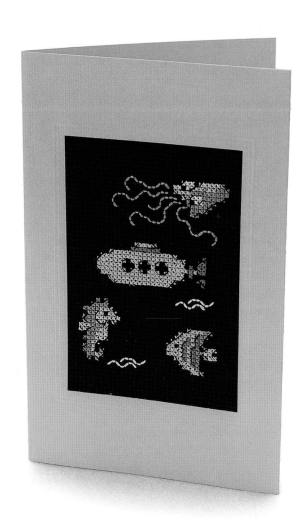

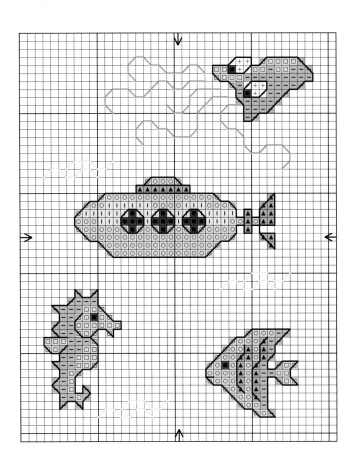

Key					
	DMC	**Anchor**		**Backstitch using 1 strand**	
+	blanc	1		**DMC**	**Anchor**
–	209	96	◣	310	403
☐	210	103			
◼	310	403		**Backstitch using 2 strands**	
⊙	726	297		**DMC**	**Anchor**
I	727	293	◪	209	96
▲	947	925	☐	747	158

Spacescape

Light up the life of your little astronaut by capturing the spirit of space adventure with this exciting card.

Measurements
The cross stitch design measures 9 x 7cm (3½ x 2¾in)

Materials
- 20cm (8in) square of navy 14-count Aida fabric
- One skein of stranded cotton in each colour listed in the key
- Size 26 tapestry needle
- Turquoise double-fold card blank measuring 11.5 x 18cm (4⅝ x 7in) with a 7.5 x 11cm (2⅞ x 4¼in) rectangular aperture

Stitch details
Cross stitch use 2 strands

Backstitch use 1 strand

Tweeded cross stitch blend a metallic thread (5272) with the other colours in the key using 1 strand of each.

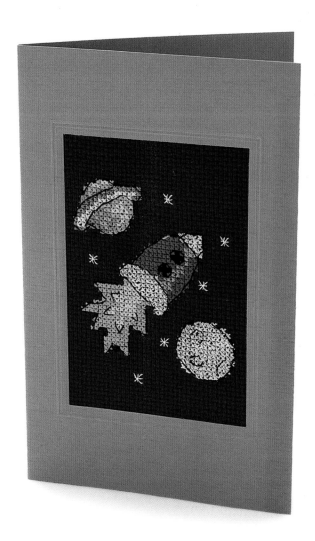

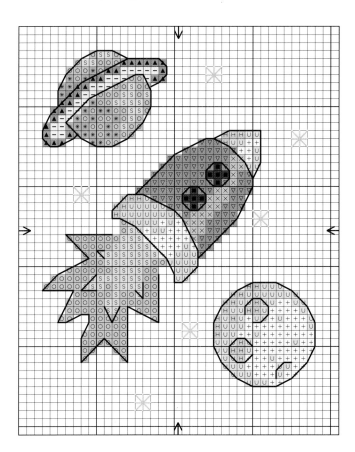

Key

	DMC	Anchor		DMC	Anchor
■	310	403	H	5272 + 318	00301 + 398
▲	553	92	U	5272 + 415	00301 + 234
S	726	297	+	5272 + 762	00301 + 397
O	741	313			
✳	947	316	**Backstitch**		
−	3078	292		DMC	Anchor
▽	3844	410	╲	310	403
✕	3846	433	╲	5272	00301

Motifs and borders

Whether you are designing a card for a would-be racing car driver or a train driver, there are suitable motifs and design components on these charts to enable you to create the perfect image. Let your imagination have free rein and use these charts as the starting point for an entirely personal design.

Key

	DMC	Anchor		DMC	Anchor
·	blanc	1	+	762	1037
N	164	264	U	800	159
S	210	342	I	813	1059
■	310	403	T	826	161
X	350	11	□	3843	410
△	352	9			
X	353	6	**Backstitch**		
▼	414	235		DMC	Anchor
O	415	234	╲	310	403
●	433	370	╲	350	11
Z	436	369	╲	414	399
−	726	295	╲	726	295
4	747	158			

Stitching equipment and charts

left: Stranded cotton has a smooth, silky texture which is perfect for cross stitching.

below: Choose a needle that is appropriate for the fabric you are using.

Fabrics

Cross stitch is generally worked on one of the evenweave fabrics, such as Aida, Hardanger, or on specialist evenweaves and linens. Aida is a specially designed fabric in which the threads are set into blocks, which give a grid-like appearance and create definite holes, making it perfect for cross stitch. Hardanger has threads woven in pairs, again creating easy-to-see holes. The specialist evenweaves and linens are loosely woven, so that you can count the threads and slide your needle between them with ease.

The fabric counts most commonly used for cross stitch are 14-count Aida and 28-count evenweave. When evenweaves are used it is usual to work each stitch over two of the fabric threads, which halves the fabric count, so that a 28-count fabric becomes the equivalent of 14-count. Fabric counts are usually calculated in inches; thus 14-count Aida has 14 blocks per inch, while a 28-count evenweave has 28 threads per inch.

To work out the finished size of a pattern, simply divide the number of stitches by the fabric count to give you a pretty accurate finished design size in inches (1in = 2.5cm). For example: when it is worked on a 14-count fabric, a motif that is 40 stitches square will measure approximately 8cm (3in) square. On an 18-count fabric, however, it will be only 6cm (2⅜in) square.

Always over-estimate the fabric size you need, leaving a couple of extra centimetres all the way round. This will allow you to secure the edges properly and leave you a

above and right: The grid-like weave of Aida makes it an ideal fabric for cross stitch.

TAPESTRY NEEDLE	FABRIC	NO. OF STRANDS
Size 26	18-count	1 strand
	16-count	2 strands
	14-count	2 strands
Size 24	11-count	4 strands
Size 22	8-count	6 strands

left: Embroidery hoops are essential for ensuring even stitching.

little leeway for mistakes and miscalculations.

Threads

Stranded cotton is probably the most widely used embroidery thread available today, and comes in a multitude of colours and shades. It is supplied as a six-stranded length, but you will generally only require a few strands at a time. The stitch details given for each project specify the number of strands to use for the various stitches used to complete a design.

Separate the strands one by one and then lay them back together in the number required. The best way to do this is to cut a length of about 45cm (18in). Hold the thread firmly between your thumb and forefinger near the top and pull one strand at a time up through your fingers and out of the bunch. Smooth the strands together between your fingers. Make sure that you do not accidentally turn any of the threads – that is, keep the 'top' cut ends together. Then thread your needle.

Needles

Tapestry needles are used for working cross stitch,

because they have blunt ends and are easily pushed into the holes of the Aida or evenweave without splitting the threads of the fabric. You will need to use a needle of an appropriate size, which depends on the fabric count and the number of strands of thread to be used. Use the table on the opposite page as a guide.

Embroidery hoops and frames

Embroidery hoops and frames come in a wide range of sizes, from a tiny 8cm (3in) hoop for small designs to large, freestanding frames for large-scale heirloom projects. Wherever possible, it is best to use a frame or hoop to keep the fabric taut while you are stitching. Not only does this help you to regulate the tension of your sewing and keep the stitches even, it also keeps the threads of the fabric straight.

Additional equipment

Other essential items to have handy when working

on your design are fabric scissors for cutting fabric and embroidery scissors for trimming threads. You may also find it helpful to use contrasting tacking thread to indicate centre marks and guidelines where necessary.

Charts

The charts in this book are easy-to-follow and beginners should have no trouble interpreting them. Each square on the chart represents one stitch. When a square is divided in half diagonally and has a tiny symbol in one or both sections, this indicates quarter and three-quarter cross stitches (see page 107 for instructions on how to form these). Backstitch is shown as a coloured line.

The charts use symbols on coloured backgrounds to indicate the different threads used. The accompanying key shows which symbol relates to which thread colour in both DMC and Anchor thread systems. In some cases, French knots and beads have been added as finishing touches and these are also listed in the keys.

The cards shown have been worked using DMC threads; the nearest Anchor equivalents are listed in each key, but if you stitch the designs using Anchor threads they may not match those shown in the pictures exactly.

below: Each design is accompanied by a clear symbol-on-colour chart.

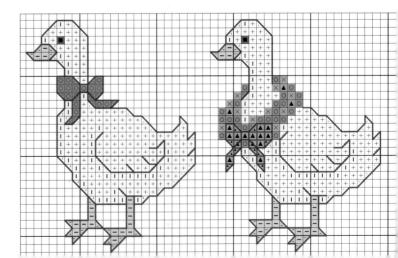

Learning to cross stitch

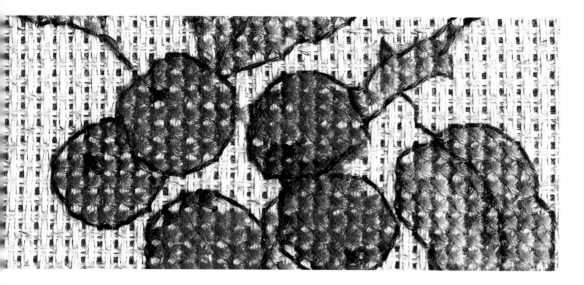

above: Designs are built up using a combination of the featured stitches.

Getting started

Cross stitch is a simple stitch to learn. It is usually worked on Aida or other evenweave fabrics. The stitch is formed from two diagonal stitches, one lying over the other, to create a cross. The stitches can be worked individually or 'row by row', when a row of diagonal stitches (or half cross stitch) is worked in one direction and then the other diagonal is stitched back over them in the opposite direction to form the crosses.

When you are working a counted cross stitch design, it is always best to start stitching from the centre of the pattern outwards. This will help to make sure that the motif is correctly positioned in the middle of the fabric. The centre of each design in

this book is indicated on the chart by arrows at the centre of each side.

To find the centre of the fabric, fold it in half vertically and then horizontally, pressing firmly on the fold to create definite creases. Open out the fabric and lay it out flat (it will now be divided into quarters by the creases), then work a line of contrasting tacking along each crease. The point at which the lines of tacking cross is the centre of the fabric.

Before you start to stitch your design, it is also a good idea to secure the fabric edges to prevent them from fraying. You can do this by hand or by binding, over-sewing or zig-zagging with a sewing machine.

Starting and finishing

Do not to use knots to start or finish a length of thread because these can create lumps and may eventually work loose or catch. Working from the front, push the needle through the fabric about 4cm (1½in) to the left of the starting point. Start stitching the first line of cross stitch, making sure you catch in the loose thread at the back. Once it is secure, pull the end through to the back. If this proves difficult, wait until you have finished that piece of stitching and then pull the end through to the back. Thread it through the needle and darn the end under a few stitches; this is also the best way to finish off.

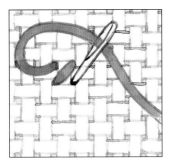

Individual cross stitch
Looking at the stitch as a square, bring the needle up through to the front of the fabric in the bottom left-hand corner and work a diagonal stitch to the top right-hand corner. Then bring the needle up through in the top left-hand corner and cross the first stitch with another diagonal stitch into the bottom right-hand corner.

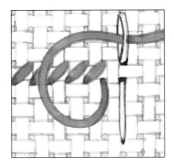

Half cross stitch
Half cross stitch is simply a single diagonal stitch. It can be worked from either bottom right to top left or bottom left to top right, depending on your preference.

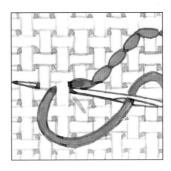

Backstitch
Backstitch can be worked in any direction and is used to outline designs and add detail. As its name suggests, the stitch is worked backwards. Work a single stitch, then bring the needle up through the fabric a stitch length ahead. Take it back down to link up the line.

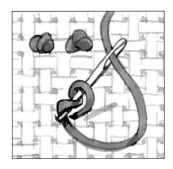

French knots
French knots are an excellent way of adding texture to your stitching. Bring the needle up through the fabric where you want the knot to be. Wrap the thread around the needle twice and pull tight (but not so tight that you cannot pass the needle through), then push the needle back down through the thread and fabric. Practise working French knots on a spare piece of fabric, as there is a knack to making them neat and even.

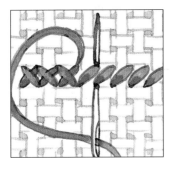

Cross stitch row by row
Bring the needle up through to the front of the fabric and work a row of diagonal stitches from top right to bottom left of adjacent squares. Then bring the needle through and work a row of diagonal stitches to cross the first ones, from top left to bottom right. You can work the rows from left to right or right to left, whichever feels most comfortable, but for a smooth, professional finish make sure that all the top stitches cross in the same direction throughout.

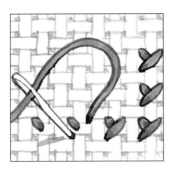

Quarter and three-quarter cross stitch
These stitches fill in half the space of a full cross stitch and give the edges of a motif a smooth line. A quarter cross stitch is simply half of a diagonal (or half cross stitch) worked from corner to middle. For a three-quarter cross stitch, work a quarter cross stitch and then work the crossing stitch diagonally from corner to corner.

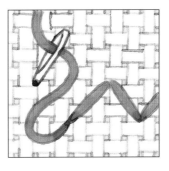

Straight stitch
Straight stitch is simply a single stitch from one point to another and is used to add detail. The stitches are usually worked on top of other stitches and can be worked in any direction. Bring the needle up through the fabric where you want the stitch to start and then take it back down where you want the stitch to finish. Make sure that all the stitches are the same size.

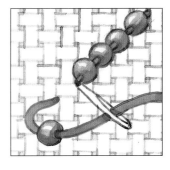

Beading
Like French knots, beading can be used to add interest to your work. Bring the needle up through the fabric where you want the bead, thread a bead on to the needle and push the needle back through the fabric. Make sure that the beads you use will thread easily over your needle.

Finishing and mounting

Aftercare

When you have finished stitching a project it can look a little creased and grubby. Most threads available today are colourfast, but do read the manufacturer's instructions before washing anything. Depending on the fabric used, you should be able to wash your work carefully by hand in warm water, using a mild detergent.

Once washed, it is best to press the stitching while it is still damp. Place the stitched piece face down on a towel which will help prevent the stitches from being flattened. Then, using a warm iron, press carefully. If the work is not completely dry afterwards, leave it flat until it is. Most embroidery fabrics have a slightly starched feel that is lost during stitching, but pressing will restore this stiffness.

below and right: A single-fold card is the simplest method of mounting, while a double-fold with an aperture can look very professional.

right: A craft knife and cutting mat are essential mounting tools.

Mounting equipment
Double-fold card blanks with aperture

These cards are available from craft and hobby stores in a wide range of colours, sizes and aperture shapes, to give a smart, professional finish to your work.

Single-fold card blanks

These are also widely available in a good range of colours and sizes, and enable you to be a little more creative when mounting your stitching.

Card, pencil and ruler

If you want to be more adventurous and make up your own cards or use a contrasting colour to create a double-mount effect, you can buy sheets of card in various colours, and it is usually cheaper than buying a couple of card blanks. You will need a pencil and ruler for marking out card templates.

Craft knife and cutting mat

A sharp craft knife or scalpel is essential when you are making your own cards and cutting apertures. A cutting mat is used to protect your table, but an offcut of thick card would do the job almost as well.

Double-sided adhesive tape

The easiest way to mount the finished stitching is with double-sided tape, which gives a secure finish but is less messy than glue.

Making cards
Single-fold card

Estimate how large you want the front of the card, then double the width (if you want the fold at the side) or the length (if you want the fold at the top). Mark the dimensions on a sheet of card and cut it out. Use a craft knife to score a line where you want the fold to be and fold the card in half.

left: A rectangular card blank can be turned to mount portait or landscape designs.

Double-fold card with aperture

Estimate how large you want the front of the card, then treble the width (if you want the fold at the side) or the length (if you want the fold at the top). Mark the dimensions on a sheet of card and cut it out. Use a craft knife to score two lines where you want the folds to be – you need to make three panels. The panel that will be folded in behind the stitching should be slightly smaller so that it will lie flat within the card. Mark out the aperture in the middle of the central panel and cut it out. Finally, fold in the panels to form the card.

Mounting the stitching

Single-fold card

Check that the finished stitching is clean and pressed, then trim the fabric to the desired size, leaving extra rows all round if you want a little fringe. Pull away the outer fabric threads to form the fringe. Stick double-sided adhesive tape to the back of the stitching around the edge, position the stitching carefully on the front of the card and, once in place, press down firmly.

Double-fold card with aperture

Check that the finished stitching is clean and pressed, then place it face down on a clean surface. Using the card aperture as a guide, estimate where the stitching will be positioned and trim the fabric so that it is slightly smaller than the front of the card. Stick double-sided adhesive tape to the inside of the card around the aperture – use several small pieces on a curved edge. With the stitching placed right side up on a clean surface, carefully position the card over the stitching and press down firmly. Stick another piece of double-sided tape along the outside edge of the panel that is to be folded in behind the stitching and fold into place.

below: A contrasting colour inserted within the aperture frames this portrait beautifully and adds an extra special finish.

Alphabets and numbers

Key

	DMC	Anchor
■	911	230
✕	913	204
−	955	202
✳	962	75
◉	3838	122

Backstitch

	DMC	Anchor
╲	911	230
╲	962	75

Traditional samplers always included names and dates in addition to the more decorative elements. Use the letters and numbers in these charts to incorporate the names or the event or occasion they celebrate. Birthday cards, too, can easily to adapted to include the age of the recipient.

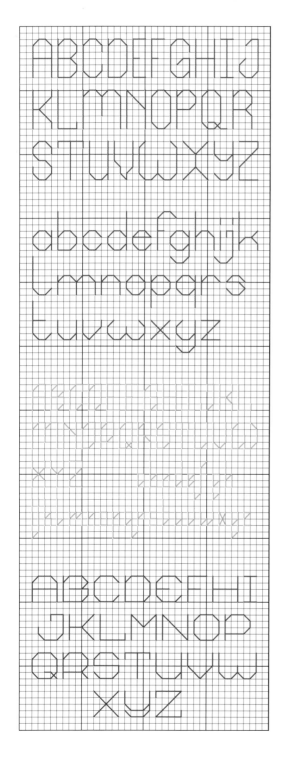

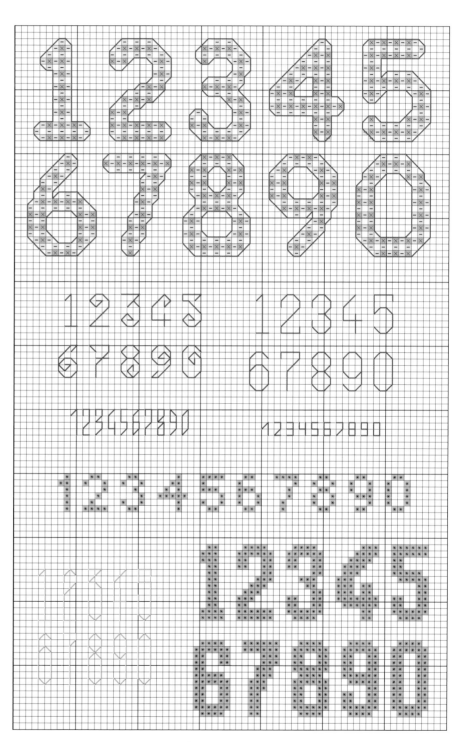

Index and acknowledgements

Executive Editor: *Doreen Palamartschuk-Gillon*
Editor: *Charlotte Wilson*
Copy Editor: *Sarah Widdicombe*
Proofreader: *Lydia Darbyshire*
Executive Art Editor: *Rozelle Bentheim*
Designer: *Ginny Zeal*
Illustrator: *Kate Simunek*
Production Controller: *Manjit Sihra*

Photography: Adrian Pope
Debi Treloar 104 top, 105 top/
Laura Wickenden 12, 13, 20, 21, 28, 35, 36, 37,
38, 44, 48, 55, 60, 61, 67, 68, 69, 92, 93, 95

With special thanks to the following people for
all their help with the stitching of the designs:
Lynda and *Claire Bowen-Davies*,
Jane Chamberlain, *Judy Davies*, *Greta*
and *Barbara Diaz*, *Michaela Learner*,
Susan Lombard, *Jo Luck*, *Angela Ottewell*,
Karen Pallett, *Glynis Smith*.

Suppliers
Craft Creations Ltd
Ingersoll House, Delamare Road, Cheshunt,
Herts EN8 9HD
Tel: 01992 781900
Fax: 01992 634339
e-mail: enquires@craftcreations.com
Web: www.craftcreations.com

DMC Creative World Ltd
Pullman Road, Wigston, Leicester LE18 2DY
Tel: 0116 281 1040
Fax: 0116 281 3592
e-mail: dmc@dmccreative.co.uk
Web: www.dmc.com

Framecraft Miniatures Ltd
Litchfield Road, Brownhills, Walsall, West
Midlands WS8 6LH
Tel: 01543 360842
Fax: 01543 453154
e-mail: sales@framecraft.com
Web: www.framecraft.com